DEDICATION

This book is dedicated to the healing
and well being of every individual
soul who is in search of becoming
more of their Authentic Self.

Sending you Love and Light.

INTRODUCTION

Allow me to start with gratitude and thanksgiving. Giving thanks for the energy that is beating my heart right now and breathing through my lungs. The eternal source that is nearer than my hands and feet and closer to me than my neck veins. I give thanks to this source, the one power, the one essence, the one love. My name is Dr. Rod, and I welcome you to the journey deep within your Soul.

This book was written with a sole intention to uplift the human spirit in order to heal and create a space for authentic self BEING. Every short writing here has the energy of unconditional love embedded within each word. These selections are written after my daily morning meditation. The majority of them have come through deep meditative thoughts and directly from my higher self. I've made it my purpose and mission in life to shift people's energies with my words.

Our words are powerful. Our words can change the world for the better. As you read this, you are being held in healing space of absolute ONENESS and kindness. Realize that my thoughts are becoming one with yours; therefore our energies are flowing together. Notice your mood.

Notice your state of mind, and notice the thoughts that are going through your awareness.

As you continue reading on with this introduction, you'll realize that your mood is shifting from a dis-empowering state into an empowering one. You are lifting yourself out of sadness and a beautiful energy of joy is going down the back of your neck, to your spinal cord, down your vertebral column, splitting into your legs and out into the ground from the bottom of your feet. Take a deep breath and allow this radiant healing energy pass through every cell of your body. At the molecular level, your cell's DNA is re-shaping itself and mending into wholeness, aligning with highest soul qualities that exist. Your energy system, the Chakra's, are becoming balanced and cleared even now, as you continue reading through this paragraph, your body is healing, your heart opening up to compassion, and your Soul dancing to the tune of the angels around, shining the light of generosity and wellness, peace and harmonizing good, creativity and genius, abundance and prosperity, beauty and bliss into every aspect of your BEING. This is what you will encounter in this book.

You can open up to any page and find a message that your Soul is yearning to get. You'll find yourself in flow with the universal life source. You'll begin to understand the secrets of your Soul, learning how to tap into the wisdom and guidance of your higher Self. I've been a student of spirituality and Truth for most of my life. I've shared my heart and soul with thousands of individuals through my social media daily, having lives changed as a result of my meditation practices and what I've dedicated my life to BE:

an intention to love, to heal, to inspire, and to be abundantly wealthy for myself and others (YOU) in order to raise the collective cosmic consciousness. I intend to heal and change the world. I intend to show the face of God as 'I AM', as Who and What I Really Am.

I've committed myself to remain humble and in service to others. This is my journey and I welcome you to walk side by side with me. I challenge you to find your purpose in life and bring out the best in you for our world.

I admire your existence and know that it is divine. You have a divine purpose and our connection in this very moment, here and now, is a testimony to your greatness. I feel your energy has been uplifted and there is a vibration of excellence flowing in your blood stream, traveling through your veins, feeding every bone, muscle, and tissue in your body. I feel happiness revealing its nature through your beautiful smile. I feel your heart opening up to love and your passion to make this world a better place pouring forth with each beat.

You are magnificent, you are powerful beyond measures, you are unique and this uniqueness shines through your AUTHENTIC BEING.

The divine in me recognizes the divine in you. Namaste.

Dr. Rod Pezeshki

ACKNOWLEDGMENTS

Special thank goes to my dear family who have always supported me on my path. My parents, Reza and Nahid. My beautiful sisters, Shadi and Shaili. My awesome brother in-laws, Kenny and Azad. Ava, Avita, and Aaron, my nieces and nephew. My new baby nephew on his way to birth, Nugget. (We don't know his real name yet). I also would like to extend my gratitude to my special friends who helped me put this book together. Thank you Ariel for choosing the subtitle. Thank you Marjan for reviewing and revising my original drafts. Thank you Rebecca, for doing an incredible job on the graphics and my editing. I appreciate your talent. You each played a unique role in the progression and manifestation of this project. I would like to thank my friend, Shayan Shidfar, for his beautiful photography on the cover page. I am grateful to all my incredible teachers, spiritual leaders, and amazing soul's who are making a big difference in our world. My special gratitude towards Dr. Michael Bernard Beckwidth from Agape International Spiritual Center. This book is published on September 17th, 2014 which marks the third year anniversary of my grandmother's passing. May her soul rest in peace. Last, I like to thank God for always showing me the light and keeping me aligned with my purpose in life.

Dr. Rod Pezeshki

ALLOW IT TO BE

Allowing others to BE Who They Are is a virtue. Especially if they are suffering for whatever reason. There are certain times that your interference with someone's experience becomes detrimental even though you are thinking you are helping them. I experienced this yesterday when I went to funeral. There was special someone in extreme distress from a loss of loved one. She didn't know what to do with her feelings. I could see so much pain and fear on her face. She was experiencing the feeling of separation from the source and the subjective attachment to this world. She needed to go through her experience and when someone told her to BE something else she was feeling, she would react very harshly. I could understand that. Why would you tell someone to BE something they are not and expect them to BE how you think they should BE? It's a question I was contemplating and staying in my space, holding a compassionate vibration where I stood next to her. The only thing I did was remaining neutral, yet internally raising my vibration into the field of unconditional LOVE. You don't have to speak or utter words for others to catch your vibration. You are part of the field of consciousness and your awareness at any precise moment is enough to bring forth healing and awakening for others.

Human emotions and thoughts are transitory. Bypass their temporary essence and you'll reach the LIGHT that embraces them collectively. As a luminous being, you are becoming more of WHO YOU ARE with every experience, catching a creative thought that comes directly from your insights through inspiration. Inspiration is an act of grace which is eternal. It always IS. It is in this IS-ness of your eternal essence that I invite you to choose your next thought, next word, and your next action. Ask:

> *Does what I say to another right now increase their awareness and empower them to BE more of their authentic self?*

Your heart will answer this question through the vibration of LOVE. Once you are aligned with it, assist. If you are not aligned with it, remain in silence.

Affirmation

"I am aligned with the inner LIGHT of my AWARENESS. I am living, moving, and having my BEING in God. I am available and receptive to more inspiration, abundance, healing, and success than I can imagine possible. Joy is the order of my day. I live with harmony and in this harmony I assist other beings to their authentic self. I live in a friendly universe, choosing to BE in the vibration of LOVE, always. In gratitude, I create my day. With passion, I sing my song to my freedom, now."

DAILY "HEART WASH"

I know you've had the experience where you've sat in your dirty car and you've told yourself: "I've got to get a car wash today". It happens all the time. You drive through the dirty window for many days until you get sick and tired of being sick and tired and do something about it. Now, remember the feeling when your car is spot less and you see through the clear window and feel fresh as you cruise happily? As we roam around this world, there is so much negative energy around, polluting the window surrounding our heart. You feel me? It happens all the time where you don't know what has hit you. If you don't pay attention to it, your emotional body will become completely obscure. Darkness takes over and the light of your heart will not be able to shine out easily.

There is a powerful energy field you can tap into and that is compassion; understanding the lack of understanding. Compassion is readily available to you when you focus on it. What it does is it clears the lens of your judgment and washes away the layers of smog, dirt, and coagulated dark energy that you've picked up from the outside world of phenomenon. Compassion penetrates through the sense of entitlement and pierces through the shell of EGO, unveiling the masks we put on daily. When you see yourself in others through the prism of compassion, you'll automatically get a daily 'heart wash' clearing you up, feeling fresh and shiny. Feeling connected and ready to wonder around this endless mesh of energy field with immense enthusiasm because you are no longer separated, no longer sitting in your inner vehicle nagging about how dirty it is.

Set your mission to feel and practice this amazing energy and exude it out to the universe today. For the world to heal, we need more compassionate people generating kindness and love.

Affirmation

"I am one with love, one with God, one with the universe. I am living, moving, and having my being in compassionate energy that exudes out of my heart. I live in a friendly universe and trust it. Life has its way through the clear vehicle of my Soul. I am available and receptive to more abundance, success, prosperity, healing and inspiration than I can ever imagine. With full on zest and overflow of kindness, I BEGIN AGAIN."

LIVING FREE

You ever notice that the very things you want to change about yourself keep showing up? Those negative aspects of your personality or the things that bother you show up out of nowhere and drive you crazy. It's a very interesting phenomenon and the more you become aware of your internal state of being, the more you'll catch this phenomenon happening. Specially, when you are concentrating on letting things go, letting previous habitual thoughts that don't serve your highest best go. I know it happens to you because it happens to me all the time, over and over again. Each time though, my reaction to my negative thoughts start losing power and my impulses as to how to deal with the challenge changes.

As you move in the direction of Self Realization and Personal Development, you become more in tune with your inner state of being. From this state of being you are becoming more of WHO you are CREATING yourself to BE. Resistant thoughts show up to be the fuel of the EGO which challenges you and tests you. Without it, you will not tap into the deeper aspects of your authentic self. The key is not to judge yourself for falling short. Realize the negative energy operating, and shine the light of transformation as you focus on the part of you that needs healing. Don't condemn it. Don't get pissed off. Be grateful because the universe is showing you which direction to go in order to expand and grow. This is a blessing in disguise.

This phenomenon happened to me yesterday. The exact opposite of what I was concentrating on and meditating on showed up like a tornado. Ohhh, I fell for it. My attitude completely shifted and my old habitual pattern expressed itself again. However, I realized which aspect of ME needs healing and Self-love. Trust and approval in myself for bypassing FEAR and standing in compete FAITH. As time passed, I cleared out this energy and felt FREE. I intend to stay this way next time the same issue shows up. When it does, I will conquer my fear and live free.

Affirmation

"I Am free in the light of trans-formation. Going beyond the form of EGO and knowing the infinite wisdom of my oneness with GOD. I am living, moving, and having my being in eternal light. I am available and receptive to more prosperity that I can ever imagine, experience, or manifest. Life supports me. LOVE is the Fuel and Funding of my SOUL. MY higher Self guides me into the path of my divine destiny. I walk in faith and peace of mind. "

IT'S NOTHING

I'm in this incredible neutral space, sitting here, having a moment of introspection and self reflection after a long meditation. Don't really know where this writing will go and don't really care at this moment because I'm totally surrender to what IS. What is, is the awesomeness of the whole, the NoThing behind everything, the No-Thing that is compared to Nothing.

As you read this, take a look at your life, where you are and where you've come from. How far you've traveled from the beginning of your existence and where is it that you are heading to. Think about all the ups and downs and pain you've endured up until this very moment. Think about all the cause and effects. Something leading to something else, then it leads into Nothing. It becomes just a memory in your head. Try to re-create the memory, try to grasp it and it will elude you. Try to grasp the Nothing, and No-thing becomes the only thing you can sense, or feel, or experience. Have you gazed at a starry sky before? Looking at the trillion stars looking back at you? What is that THING that's looking back at you? Take a deep breath right now. Feel the space between your two eyes, your two ears, and the space between your two shoulders. Take another breath, go down into your heart, the space between your chest cavity and lungs. Another deep breath, and feel the space between your heart chambers. As it fills up with blood with your next pulse, it goes into a cycle of NO-THING and NOTHING. Then, there is a gap that includes both the NOTHING and

EVERYTHING. This is the void that includes it all. This gap is right now connecting the thought impulses in your mind, your breath, the fibers of your entire being, your cells, emotional experiences, memories, and the awareness of what you are reading, comprehending. The stars you looked at are the out picturing of the mind of God, the universe birthed from NO-THING, yet becoming everything as YOU, your life, your entire being. They are a reflection of YOU. You've been always unfolding throughout eternity as the expression of No-Thing and NOTHING, re-created into everything in order for NO-thing to experience itself. You and No-thing are one and the same. There is only ONE-Thing and that is love. You are LOVE.

Affirmation

"I surrender to No-thing to manifest as everything in my life. Cosmic ideas take form and grow in the garden of my consciousness. I Am one with Everything and Nothing can inhibit my love. Joy is the order of my day. I am abundantly fueled and connected to harmonizing prosperity manifesting as the miracles in my life."

RECIPE FOR PEACE

How can you describe color to a natural born blind person? It's very challenging, yet there are other sense perceptions that become activated and sensitized throughout the person's growth given the right 'conditions' to function normally in life and have a significant life. The world we live in is the projection of previous 'THOUGHT' perceptions of our collective consciousness. Manifesting as what it is. The experience of it is "TRANSITORY". It comes with different flavors, some distasteful such as the current events you hear, experience, and witness. Yet there is the "OPTIMIST" side of it. The side that is striving for "PEACE" and holding the space for it. How do you change? How can you have an active participation in a spiritual principal that is not just a rhetoric, it's Real. Perhaps this is the only Reality that exists. Yet, we've been hijacked by our own Ego's and been fed negativity through different channels for profit, war, personal gains, hate, and bigotry.

Peace is an inner state of being on an individual basis. Doesn't matter who you are, where you are, and what your previous experience has been. It does require an intention to bring it forth. Realize I'm saying to bring it forth, not creating it. Peace already exists, it's an ETERNAL quality. Having the willingness is the first criteria which will lead you to forgiveness. Forgiveness will open the gateway to compassion, which is understanding the lack of understanding. Once you are there, courage shows up as your inherent virtue. With courage you can love unconditionally. This is the KEY that will make you a catalyst for change. Change in what? A real change not based on your previous held thoughts, emotions, experiences of fear and lack. A change in real thought that cause a change in your daily conversation. Once your conversations starts changing, your agreement about these high conversation changes. A collective agreements of masses of people who have these high intention to forgive, find their portal to compassion through courage and tap in their unconditional love for the entire humanity will bring forth peace in the world. This is not a DREAM. It's Reality into MAKING. Now, it's your choice! Choice is the function of your awareness, and your awareness is the function of your spiritual practice.

Affirmation

"I am living, moving, and having my being in LOVE. In God I reside and move forth in faith. My Soul is activated with the power of peace and has the willingness to be a catalyst for change. I am available and receptive to more abundance than I can imagine, experience, or manifest. I trust the universe. I AM an affirmatory optimist with life. "

I AM FREE

Have you ever had a conversation with the Angel of Death?
I did yesterday. It was a special communion with this
phenomenon we call death. I visited a friend of mine in the
hospital yesterday. He had a stroke about 7 month ago and
he's physical body has been depreciating ever since.
Struggling with life, laying in bed, having a G. Tube to get
fed, and has half his body paralyzed. He's around 80 and a
really cool guy. I remember when I was a kid, I used to
wrestle with him and tease him around because he
despised a certain vegetable. So, anytime we called the
name of this vegetable (Shalgham) he'd make facial
gestures and we'd laugh at him. So, here we were
yesterday, my friend on the bed, I was holding his hand and
massaging his shoulder. All I felt was his bones. His muscles
were totally gone. He'd come in and out of consciousness as
he would open his eyes, gaze at me, and with all his power
would give me a smile. I'd continued asking him questions,
especially those that would trigger his memory from the
past and have him remember some of the pleasurable
events. He'd remember and squeeze my hand. Then, fall
back to sleep until few minutes later to open his eyes again.
In the midst of my physical encounter, I was beholding him
in the presence of God. Bypassing my Ego, I'd see him as
whole, perfect, and complete. I felt myself becoming an
energy field of consciousness, surrounding his body in
different shades of colors, going in and out of his Chakras.
I'd look above his crown Chakra and see a halo. As I was
holding this healing space for him, I'd have tons of insights

with angel of death. I saw his face in disguise, showing up as physical changes in my friend's fragile body. Giving me lessons about how to appreciate life and let go of fear because everything eventually belongs to God. From your most precious possessions all the way to your physical health, essentially your entire life. It all belongs to God.

As I was having moments of self Realization, I was thinking about the times that I get into arguments with my loved ones. Times that we take for granted and hurt each other. Times that we could stay in gratitude and enjoy, yet we totally forget who and what we are. We blindly go in resentment and quarrel. If my friend would want to continue writing this note, he'd say something like this: *"Listen to the tune of your heart, love each other, and don't take your happy moments for granted. Live full on with vigor! Live full on with every ounce of your energy in serving and loving each other through kindness. Be a giver rather than a taker. Give off your blessings everywhere you go and enjoy. When the time comes to face the angel of death, look at it without fear. Be proud that you lived a life of significance as your legacy will echo into eternity"*...I AM FREE.

Affirmation

"I am living, moving, and having my being in love. My life is the life of God. I am grateful for all of my blessings and share it with others. I intend to be kind and caring, allowing for life to flow through me. I let go, forgive, and stay in peace. The universe supports me and I trust it. Abundance is the order of my day. Harmonizing prosperity and healing reign supreme. I begin again, now, and so it is, Amen."

WHITE FLAME

Illuminating your mind requires surrendering, meaning "I am available to what seeks to emerge through and as me". Are you ready for this illumination? If you wish to continue with this, let go of the past thoughts you are holding about yourself. If you don't wish to continue, simply smile and send out a blessing to the world. As you take a deep breath, allow the flow of the universal presence move through you. Let the oxygen feed every cell in your body and relax into the moment. I don't know where you are, I don't know what you are doing. What I know is that you've read this far and there is a deep connection beyond your mental conception of what these words are saying. There is a knowing that has nothing to do with your logic. It has something to do with the love in your heart. The energy that you are feeling is unconditional love. The only thing that IS. It's your essence, it's what will illuminate your mind and go beyond the rough edges of previous held thoughts you've been dealing with. Anything that does not support you from the past will disappear in the next few moments.

Imagine now you are standing all alone in front of the ocean. You are breathing deep and feeling the soft wind coming from the waves. As you connect to your breath, you'll feel the inflow of your breath completely synchronized by the rise of the wave. When you exhale, the waves become one with the ocean itself. Feel the sun light covering your body, feeling the heat that's being generated.

As you focus on your breath, feel the sun rays becoming infinite WHITE FLAMES, an energy field that is stemming from your heart, surrounding your physical body, It's intensity is increasing as you breath, with each wave of the ocean flowing inside. With its own mighty power through your breath, you feel the intensity of the white flame increase. It starts taking over the deepest component of your cellular structure, going through your blood stream, inside your brain cells. Be aware of the thought behind your thought now, and the thought beyond your thought. See the White Flame dancing in the spaces in between your thoughts. It moves through peacefully and clears out any past painful experiences. It stretches your paradigm and shifts your mental conception about our universe. It allows infinity find its way through the portal of your thought. Possibilities are showing up as ways appearing out of no way. As your life's vision becoming more apparent by your higher Self, your life experience is easing up. Challenges are fading away within the White Flame. Love is gushing through the spaces in between your cells. There is a peaceful energy passing through you right now. Do you feel It? Simply Be with this and enjoy the moment. Carry this energy with you the entire day. Each time you experience sadness, fear, worry, and disappointment, simply go within and turn on your mental illumination with the White Flame of love, of joy, of infinite abundance, of inspiration and hope. You are being guided and loved right now. Fear is dissolved. Once again, we are becoming as ONE.

Affirmation

"I am living, moving, and having my being in total acceptance. I flow with LOVE and have my thoughts in peace. I am an eternal being of love. My power comes from within. I am available and receptive to more abundance and success than I can ever imagine, experience, or manifest before. My life is the life of God. Today, I joyfully exercise my right to shine and be a blessing to the world."

VICTIM NO MORE!

Victim no more my friend! I'm not a victim of my emotions anymore. I'm not a victim of what other people think about me or what I think what others think about me anymore. The journey from victim to victor is a beautiful path. It begins with taking one hundred percent responsibility for your life. For your happiness, for you joy. Responsibility is the ability to respond to the lesser Egoic thought patterns and recognizing the negative energies surrounding you. Responsibility creates the possibility for change to express. In what areas of your life you feel you were a victim of society, of someone else's hatred, or a situation that completely hurt you? I'm sure you've experienced something at this level or experiencing it now perhaps. Let me tell you this: VICTIM NO MORE! You are waking up to your greatness and in that greatness there is power in you.

There is a genius lying dormant, a spiritual warrior armed with her optimism, armed with courage, armed with her inner attitude of gratitude. You are backed up by the universe and collective consciousness of people who care about you. There are kind people out there, loving beings who are ready to support you. Your time to being a victim is over! You are rising up and releasing the pain you've been holding on in your heart. You are becoming the victor and feeling the victory in every breath you are taking. It begins with this very decision you are making now. SAY:

I'M NOT A VICTIM ANYMORE. NOT A VICTIM TO MY FEELINGS, THOUGHTS, OR EMOTIONS. I'M A UNIQUE CHILD OF THE UNIVERSE AND I ALLOW MY OWN SPIRITUAL POWER TO LIFT ME OUT OF THE PAIN I'VE BEEN CARRYING. I HEAL THE PAST WOUNDS! I AM FREE. I AM LIBERATED!

Affirmation

"I am living, moving, and having my being in God. I am a victor and feel victorious in every area of my life. I move with confidence. I attract abundance and success in my life. I exude love energy everywhere I go. I am courageous and strong. My faith is crystal clear. I am available to more good than I can imagine possible in my life. I trust the universe and exercise optimism within my Soul."

TIME

Identifying with Time is the root of anxiety. You know what I'm talking about? The beginning of the week, or getting to the middle of the year, looking at yourself and identifying with your chronological age, looking in the mirror seeing the gray hair and identifying with old age. All of these mental constructs that enable us to compartmentalize the world of material into functionality can create a sense of inner anxiety. Take a deep breath in this very now, the only moment ever existed and ever will be. Step out of your mental construct and anxiousness with time, let go of it. View this day as a moment in eternity. Think of the sun for a second. Imagine its beautiful energy laying on your skin. Do you really think the sun cares about time? It's always on to its own nature, shining, giving energy and doing it's thing. Think of the ocean and it's waves for a second. Do you think it cares about TIME? It's always BEING its own nature, in tune with the harmony of the universe. You are made up of elements of the stars, energy of the cosmos vibrates through you. You can measure and experience time for the sole purpose to go beyond it. It's a reverse process, to re-member what you've forgotten. Take this on today. Step outside time and re-cognize the eternal aspect of yourself. No end, no beginning, always IS. Now, get rid of your watch today, try it, and don't look at your phone or anything that reminds you of time. Stay focused on your breath as you do whatever you do and see how everything you are up to will ease up. You will flow from the timeless essence of your higher self and remain in presence. This is where peace resides. Shift your energy from hurry to slowing down and you'll experience the peace you've been searching for from within.

Affirmation

"I am eternal. I am love. I am living, moving, and having my being in the now. My life is the life of God. I am available and receptive to more abundance than I can ever imagine. Life affirms itself through the beauty of my soul. My heart is wide open to express its purpose for revealing the divine through my thoughts, words, and actions today, in the now. I am grateful and thankful for NO-THING that shows up as everything my Soul requires to achieve its purpose. I trust the universe and flow through it with ease."

BEING IN AWE

I just came out of an amazing meditation. Listening to a beautiful Native American music. I had time travel in my meditation. It's quite an amazing experience. Feeling and seeing yourself as everyone and everything. The closest way I can describe ONENESS is through the sense of love. The way to experience this is through appreciation and awe. Take a deep breathe and let this thoughts come through what you are reading here and allow it to simply flow with your breath. Focus on the in-flow of your breath. At the end of the inhalation, make a conscious pause for a second or two, then gently allow the out-flow, effortlessly. Continue reading and relaxing. Let it all go. I know you are feeling in tune with what I'm writing. Otherwise you wouldn't have read this far. Continue visioning a beautiful mountain with all the trees, rocks, and its inhabitants. Feel your breath connected to the flow of energy through the trees and the rocks. The roots of the trees, getting nourishment from the soil, finding their connection in the darkness of the ground, connected to the soul of the mountain. Travel up from the roots, up to the branches and the leaves. Feel the fresh air touching the surface of the leaves. Breathing in oxygen from the leaves, exhaling tension out in the open. Feel the sun sitting on the leaf. It's like a beautiful rug, covering the surface with its beautiful design, the photons dancing around a fire pit to the tune of the wind, the leaf shaking from its base. As this is happening, see yourself as the eagle sitting on this branch. Noticing what's happening with the leaf, the wind, and the sun. She's connecting to the root, the soil, and the mountain itself. In awe and appreciation of life, she takes off by opening her wings. Feeling the freedom of expanding beyond her space. Her role as a peace keeper and paradigm changer expands as she encounters the ocean. With her dark brown eyes, she observes the dolphins dancing with the waves, expressing their affection to the sun as they rise above the crest and send out the kiss to the eagle. Each breath you are taking now is in sync with harmony of natural laws of the universe. This law stems from love and its opposing polarity is fear. You are meant to experience and live in love, because that's your true nature, your authentic self. The opposing pole is a way to let you know that you are getting distance from your source. Fear creates an illusion and this illusion becomes obsolete as you become in AWE of the natural order of the universe. Look inside my friend, you've read this far and have become one with your SOUL. As you take this last conscious breath, know that you are in my prayers and know that the POWER OF LOVE will guide you to what is exactly meant for your greatness, a divine destiny unveiling itself as your life, in this very moment.

Affirmation

"My life is the life of God. I am living, moving, and having my being in love. I am available and receptive to more prosperity, abundance, success, and wealth than I can imagine possible. Healing break through every area of my life. My relationships are in harmony with joy. Peace shows it's face everywhere I go. The energy of cosmic good seeks expression through me. I let it. I allow, I let go. I AM."

CLARITY OF PERCEPTION

Clarity of perception. That's what it's all about. How you
view things and at what depth can you experience life.
Everyone's perception is unique. We all have different ways
of re-presenting cosmic order according to our gifts. Your
DNA is a direct evidence of this Truth. Nothing the same.
Can you really grasp the immensity of how great you are?
No, really? When you step beyond what your physical eyes
and perception can see, you can catch the vibration of
eternal qualities that are within you. I was with a client of
mine yesterday. She is absolutely an incredible person.
Caught in the lower frequencies of the external
circumstances just like every one of us. At the moment we
were navigating through different spiritual principals, I
could see a shift of perception happening through her eyes.
It is as if you've been seeing through clouds, a morning fog.
Then, suddenly rays of sun light show up and twinkle
through your eyes. For me it's the most beautiful thing to
witness trans-formation and experience this shift in
consciousness. As clarity overcomes the shadows of our
EGO, life begins to show its REAL face through the
authenticity of your Soul. Everything starts feeling and
looking different. There is a bliss factor operating naturally
without any kind of addiction to the high. It's just there. It's
palpable, as real as your heart beat. Effortlessly showering
you with love through its presence. You have a great destiny
not determined by your past Karma. Remember that karma
could only determine a circumstance appearing to you as
your reality. It can be shifted and overcome through your

attitude, your resilience for greatness. Your attitude of love, peace, compassion, and gratitude will determine your destiny. You have a divine destiny waiting for your willingness to say YES to it.

Affirmation

"I trust my destiny because I trust the universe. I am living, moving, and having my being in unconditional love. My perception is clear and each day becomes more aligned with the fundamental order of the universe. I am available for more abundance than I can ever imagine. Life reveals its secrets to me through nature. I am aligned with my Soul's authenticity. With a heart full of joy and eyes full of cosmic energy, I begin this eternal journey."

BEYOND APPEARANCE

Here is something I've learned over the years; "Don't ever assume what is best for other people." There is so much you don't know about them. Each person has a unique characteristic and has a gift deep within their soul regardless of what they are growing or going through in their life. Become a passive observer and hold a space for love when you see them in pain. As you remain low and humble, emulating the great oceans of our planet, other river streams will flow to you because you are staying open and receptive rather that giving 'ADVICE' to them. When you encounter someone who is experiencing drama, ask yourself:" What is the meaning of what appears to BE?" Don't jump into sudden judgment because that's the trap of the Ego. You can totally heal others by being present to your own thoughts and at the moment the temptation of "I KNOW BETTER THAN" crawls into your mind, say to yourself: WHAT IS THE MEANING OF WHAT APPEARS TO BE? There is a hidden answer in every challenging circumstance that will reveal it's true face when you become in tune with the fundamental order of the universe. I'm sending my love and blessing to people who are witnessing their loved ones in pain, or those who are going through very difficult times themselves. Hang on, go beyond what you are caught up in, and stay in tune for deeper understanding of what's being revealed to you through the challenge at hand. Ask your Soul for assistance. You will receive divine guidance and a solution for it.

Affirmation

"I am grateful and thankful for all the blessings in my life. I'm living, moving, and having my being in love. The universe guides me and gives me directions as I take on my incarnation fully. I am available and receptive to more abundance and success than I can ever imagine. I live in flow. I move in peace. I talk and act in accordance to the order of the universe. Joy is breaking out in every area of my life. Healing is revealing it's beautiful face in my heart and emanates its powerful aura everywhere I go. I am in tune with my song and sing it all day long."

I DON'T KNOW!

Do you want to move from being self-centered into becoming centered in the Self? I'm talking about having a stronger connection with your higher Self and stepping out of your Ego. It's very possible and it requires your attention to your inner world. It requires knowing that YOU DON"T KNOW. Simple ha? Have you noticed people that play as if they know it all? You've experienced that person and sometimes you've fallen for your own mask of I KNOW IT ALL. Well, now that you know you DON"T KNOW, it's a great space to BE. It's an awareness that will simplify your life. Through Simplicity, you become expansive, and through expansion of your consciousness, the wisdom of the universe finds its way for expression through the vibration of your thoughts. You become an instrument of peace and love. These two are not knowing, they are eternal qualities of being. You just began a process of Self Realization, a change from being self centered to becoming centered in the Self. Take a deep breath and make this your intention today: "I DON'T KNOW ANYTHING and from KNOWING NOTHING , I tap into the mystery of life, thus downloading cosmic wisdom through my intuition now." I can feel and sense the freedom you are feeling for not KNOWING. Let it go. You know! Step in the UNKNOWN my friend through your faith and loving intention.

Affirmation

"I know that I don't KNOW. In the space of not KNOWING, I become available and receptive to the all good. My life is the emanation of the only one life that exists. Love is my nature, peace is my song. I am living, moving, and having my being in God. Joy is the order of my day. I am available to more abundance and prosperity than I can ever imagine. Life supports me. Healing is revealing it's beautiful face to me in every area of my life. And so it is, Amen."

YOUR CALLING IS CALLING YOU

Listen, something has been calling you. So many times you told yourself I'm going to change, I'm going to do that thing that gets me excited, gets me really happy. However, for whatever reason, you shut yourself down. How many of you guys relate to this? You are living yet you keep on leaving your heart's desire. You are living but you are waiting to get somewhere in the future to finally do the thing you are meant to do and BE the person you are meant to Be. In this very moment, think about it. I know there is something underneath your mind, if we sit together, you'll whisper it in my ears. You'll say:

> *"I am more than this! I am meant for greatness! I know I have powers deep in my Soul that carry me through the challenges I'm facing right now! I also know that these adversities are creating the right conditions for the tiny acorn to manifest into its maximum potential. Being and Becoming the mighty oak tree."*

I know you've got it in you. I just know it and you can't BS around with me because I'm not talking to your excuses, your old belief systems, your complaints and nagging. I'm talking directly to your Soul and activating an awareness that is beyond what you can see or what you can hear. There is a field of pure potentiality that is invisible yet indivisible from you. YOU are it and IT is you. Thus, in this moment, I'm praying you up to align you with your divine purpose. Becoming who you are truly meant to be. Open your heart and accept this gift. As you do, hold on to that inner voice, contemplate and meditate on it. Your purpose is calling you. Are you going to answer the call?

Affirmation

"I am one with life, one with love, one with the universe. My calling is calling me and I'm activating my potential right now. I'm picking up on my calling and allowing life to overflow its abundance through me, as me, as my life, as my words, my actions, and my thoughts. I am available and receptive to more good than I can possibly imagine. Healing is the order of my day. Joy is my middle name. Bliss is all that I see. Prosperity showers my entire being with love and peace vibrates through every cell of my body."

IT'S EASY, YET IT'S HARD

You wonder what I'm talking about? I don't even know yet as I'm getting in a zone to just write. It's one of those states of being that I feel my creative urge overflowing with insights. My heart is racing and my mind is wondering to so many places. I'm actually very present, in the moment. I'm very present to my feelings. I feel every cell in my body vibrating. My hands are actually shaking at a very subtle level. It's a strange space to be, yet for me it's a very pleasant place because I feel free in this moment. Free from the confinements of my mind, having my heart rule. My heart Chakra is widely open and feels the vibration of the universe. The Ohmm sound of creation echoing in my ear drums. It's easy to get lost in your own thoughts sometimes. Not being in flow, then it becomes hard to deal with everyday challenges. Can you relate? Have you noticed the times when you hurt a loved one without really meaning it? Not having control over your impulses and all of the sudden hell breaks loose? You then get into this feeling of regret. Regret is very powerful and dense. It sucks the living energy out of you. If you are a sensitive being, you may carry its residues for many hours unless you give yourself a chance to introspect, go deep down in your heart, and clear this energy out. It's easy to fall prey to your Ego, yet it's hard to keep yourself together in peace and harmony. It's easy to stay in ignorance and ignore your connection to ONENESS, yet once you feel the feeling of being connected, it's hard to forget. It's easy to be in love, yet when you get used to the feeling of being in love, it's hard to maintain it. You may take it for granted and forget what allowed you to be in love in the first place. Life is full of surprises and ups and downs. It's easy to witness these surprises, yet it's hard to believe that every surprise is synchronized for your own evolution. The evolution of the Soul. It's easy to deny your Reality and fall into abyss, into an empty space, into the dark matter that easily pulls you down and disconnects you from the source. The hard part is knowing that this is happening to you. The hard part is surrendering to the Truth. Knowledge becomes resistance. The more you know sometimes becomes your own worst enemy for becoming available to witness the Truth. To experience the Truth. I feel every breath going in and out of my lungs right now. The heat and the tingling in my hands are getting more intense. I can see my Soul floating above my physical body and expanding beyond this space. It's easy to be in joy of recognizing your divinity, yet it's hard to be aware of this all the time. The pull and push of the energies outside sometimes gets the best of us. That's why practicing what you believe becomes your bread, your water. It becomes the nutrient that feeds your brain and feeds your organ system. Why am I writing this I don't know. Maybe there is a hidden message that wants to resonate through me and find its way to you. Maybe there is something you need to hear that will expand and create space within your heart to become more than who you are. Maybe it's just an escape right now for me, allowing me to cope with my feelings. It's easy for me to write, whether or not I'm making sense, however it's hard to express what I'm feeling. It's hard to describe that which is not describable. Have you ever had a dream where you were awake in your dream? You witness yourself in the dream without being part of the dream. As if you are an extension of something bigger. Now, has this happened to you when you are awake? If so, next time you get in this situation ask yourself am I dreaming in my awake state or am I truly awake in my dream state? The answer is up to you. It's up to you to perceive how you want to perceive it. It's easy to fall down and blame everybody else for your fall, yet it's hard to accept that you are not alone on this journey, that once you fall down, the cycle of life will support you to get back up. It's hard to accept this right? Yet it's easy to yield to it. If I've driven you crazy by now, it's easy for me to ask forgiveness. Because in the act of For-giveness, I'm giving you something beyond what your conscious mind is able to accept, or pick up. It's easy to infuse my love through these words and inoculate you with a high energy that I'm feeling. Yet, it's hard for me to not feel the blood flow in your body, getting more intense, becoming livelier, more passionate, and more alive. As I leave you with this note, my prayer is for expansion of your thoughts, blessing you through unconditional love, knowing that in this very moment you and I are ONE. I hold you in the secret place of the most high, where you can only experience peace and love. YES, It's easy to SEE you as you ARE, yet it's hard to stop loving you because we are ONE.

Affirmation

"I am living, moving, and having my being in God. Love is my name and is my nature. I am available and receptive to more good than I can possibly imagine. Healing is the order of my day. Abundance and prosperity are showing their face everywhere I go. I live in a field of infinite possibilities for fulfilling my purpose. I am aligned with my divine destiny. Life supports me."

SHAMANIC DANCE

One day at a time my friend. Don't lose HOPE. I was speaking to someone yesterday who is going through a very challenging time. At a physical level, she is experiencing severe pain and at an emotional level, she has lost hope. Lost faith in everything. We went into a deep conversation and she realized that her pain is being caused indirectly by her lack of love towards herself and the thirst to get others approval in order to feel whole. I asked if she has faith in nature? Forget about religious dogmas and scripts, I asked if she had faith in the Sun, in the Moon, in her own heart beat, in the next breath creating the energy necessary for her survival. It's amazing when the depth of your conversation shape shifts negative energy and uplifts someone regardless of what they are experiencing. Healing is a direct result of your own willingness and faith in your higher self. One day at a time, starting with today, take a stand for loving yourself and approving of yourself. Take a stand for courage. It takes courage to go beyond the negative pull of the society, circumstances, and past experiences. It takes courage to get into the momentum of creativity, opening your heart for selfless action. Going beyond what you think is possible for you, beyond other peoples expectation of you, beyond what your limiting belief systems has tied your spirit up with. I know you are courageous. I feel it from sitting here in my little writing/meditation space right now. I've intended this for you. Hope, Faith, and Courage right NOW. It's been activated already automatically through every breath you are taking. Did you notice your next breath right now? Yes? You can smile and laugh. That was Faith, Hope, and Courage riding the oxygen molecules carried to your lungs, to your heart, then swimming in your blood stream and doing their Shamanic dance into trillions cells of your body. As you are in this healing space, the course of your day will shift and will ripple out to the world for a big change. Anytime you feel discouraged and hopeless, remember the Shamanic dance floating in your blood stream with each breath.

Affirmation

"I am one with God, one with love, one with the Universe. All of my needs are met. Everything happens for my higher good. I am available and receptive for more abundance and prosperity than I can imagine possible. Healing is the order of my day. I am receptive to wisdom and guidance directly from my over Soul. Life supports me in divine right action. In gratitude, I take the next breath and do my Shamanic dance with tons of love in my heart."

YOUR LIFE MATTERS!!

You matter, your thoughts matter, your life matter. Every breath you take matters. The life you are living matters to the entire world. Your vision matters. What is the creative vision of your Soul? What are you here to do? I know you've asked yourself this question. The process of asking this question opens up portals from the deepest state of your being and downloads intuitive guidance directly from your over soul in order to pull your Divine Vision into manifestation. Your every thoughts matters to the evolution of our consciousness.

Today, the world needs more spiritual warriors, people who engage in higher conversations, who are kind and loving, who operate from state of cooperation and unity, and who are compassionate in order for healing to happen. Operating at this level requires your agreement to excellence, not perfection. That excellence is cultivated from accepting who and what you are, the way it is, and increasing your capacity to grow spiritually through constant practice, commitment, discipline. This is your Soul's mandate. You are not here to waste your incarnation. You are here to be channel for trans-forming our world. Yes! You matter, your thoughts matter, your life matter! If for a second you thought otherwise, you are walking in a dream state. You are not awaken to your higher truth. You have not yet opened your eyes beyond your eyes. Seeing life through the prism of light and love. Feel this energy vibrating and lifting you up because today, your life is about to change to excellence. YES, YOU ARE NOT WAITING ANY LONGER! Today is your day...Because: YOU MATTER, YOUR THOUGHTS MATTER, YOUR LIFE MATTERS!

Affirmation

"I am living, moving, and having my being in excellence. I am available and receptive to more abundance, success, health, wealth, happiness, peace, love, prosperity, healing, and joy than I can even imagine possible. The universe guides and supports me. I am grateful and thankful for NO-THING that manifests into miracles in every areas of my life."

VIRTUE

Fear is the byproduct of "the need to control". Let go of the need to control others and trust the process of Life. There is a hidden virtue in the nature of existence, an eternal force that's breathing through you right now, closer than your neck veins, nearer than your hands and feet. How often do you contemplate its existence and how often do you doubt yourself being separate from it? In the moment you break into separation, you open the gates of negative energy into your energy field. Why? Because, you are in judgment. Judgment of us versus them, me versus you, or the envious longing to have what they've got which dis-connects you from the hidden virtue and pulls you in the madness of the world. Simplify your life. Let go of arriving somewhere in the future and yield to the now.

TOMORROW

Tomorrow, you will think back of today realizing your choices and actions you could have made that could have had major significance. A choice to be kinder, a choice to be more loving, a choice to share more of your blessings with others. A choice to be appreciative, and a choice to be humble. Every breath you take in the now is a blessing from the divine. Your every thought comes from the presence that is never an absence, an intelligence that needs your awareness for embracing it, for embodying its characteristics as yourself from the core of your inner being.

I know you've experienced what I'm talking about here, because I know you've stood in front of the mirror and gazed into your own eyes before. The Soul can be seen from the window of your eyes and can be felt in the silent moment of meditation. Tomorrow, you'll think back at this very moment and realize that something was shifted in you. An inspiring flow of energy that made you think of your greatness, a shift in your attitude towards your next step. An expansion in your perception. A commitment to excellence without getting caught up in judgment or drama. Stay in grace my friend. You are doing well. Tomorrow, you will look back at today and say: I AM GRATEFUL FOR MY DAY.

Affirmation

"I am living, moving, and having my being in love. All of my needs are met. I am available and receptive to more abundance, prosperity, success, joy, health and happiness than I can imaging possible. I live in the NOW moment. I am full of zest for life. I attract and allow infinite plentitude and beauty in my life because that's who I am. I am blessed and a blessing in the world. I live a purposeful life with passion with every breath I take."

SWEEP ME AWAY

There is always a pain inside our hearts no matter what we do to keep it out of our body. This is an emotional pain. The intensity of it doesn't matter because for some is very mild, for some it's very strong. I have days that I feel the pain of the world in my heart and transmute this energy somehow into an act of kindness towards others. You know exactly what I'm talking about. Sometimes, this pain shows up as fear, sometimes as guilt, sometimes as anxiety, and sometimes as sadness. If you don't acknowledge it, it turns into madness because it has an Egoic root to it from the madness of the world. As you read this, follow the energy coming through me right now and for the next few seconds stay present to your thoughts. I'm writing a longer post to fine tune your attention on the intention behind the words coming through me. This intention is healing the pain that has manifested in your physical, emotional, or collective body. Take a deep breath: Follow the path of your breath all the way down to your lower back, in between your vertebral column, through your spine. Hold it for a few seconds. Exhale out. Do this again. Slowly become present to the breath. As you do this, imagine a beautiful caterpillar nesting in your heart. With each breath, the oxygen you are sending your heart is feeding the trillion of cells in your body and sending waves of loving, healing energy through the molecules of your blood stream. It is feeding the caterpillar, who is in a dormant stage, holding on to lower energies before becoming free. Breath in, witness the dissolution and mutation of the caterpillar into a most beautiful butterfly you've ever seen. Feel your heart beat, feel the next breath you are taking transmuting the pain into healing, depression into joy, anxiety into peace, and scarcity into abundance. The source behind the creation of all eternity is invisible yet it is indivisible from you. You are the source of your own healing. Now, notice the butterfly opening up its wings and with your next breath traveling throughout your entire body, getting deep down at sub-molecular, DNA level, clearing out any old, stagnant residues of fear, guilt, shame, and blame with it. It's sweeping out your inner household and assisting you into a field of trans-formation. Notice it multiplying, and with the next breath out, all of them leaving your energy field. As they surround you in a beautiful circular motion, they change colors from red to orange, yellow, green, blue, purple, and a golden white spheres of high frequency vibration. At this time, if you've read this far, you are being activated into healing energy of Reiki with an intention for healing, harmonizing prosperity, divine guidance, wisdom, abundance, and purpose for your life. Take a deep breath, hold it, hold it, hold it: Say:

"ALL OF MY NEEDS ARE MET, EVERYTHING HAPPENS FOR MY GOOD, LIFE SUPPORTS ME. I FORGIVE AND LET GO , I LET GO AND LET GOD. I AM WHOLE, PERFECT AND COMPLETE. I AM HEALED. I AM BLESSED AND A BLESSING TO THE WORLD. MY LIFE IS DIVINE. IN GRATITUDE, I TAKE MY NEXT BREATH IN LOVE AND JOY."

... Exhale out. God bless you.

RELATIONSHIPS

Relationships come and go. Just like any other cycles of life, not everyone that meets and commits to a traditional man made concept of marriage or binding contract stay together, forever. In the course of your life, you go through growth and expansion. There is a quantum field of infinite possibility that is present at every moment. When you meet the conditions for expansion, that which already exist in the universe become manifested in your reality. A lot of times when people are going through this spiritual growth, awakening, and Realization, what happens is that their partners or significant others are too stuck in the lower frequencies. Stuck in their Ego. Stuck in the societal expectations of mediocrity and herd consciousness. Meaning that they follow the masses and don't have an intuitive vision of who they are, what they are, and what their purpose is in their lives. They become so identified with material world, their names, status, title, car they drive, zip code they live in, and type of shoes they wear that Real meaning of their lives becomes obsolete. What happens then is, the other partner starts living in another Reality. In joy consciousness. In oneness. In love. In another paradigm. People separate because at each moment, there is a completion of a lesson taught by another soul in your life and the cycle of expansion and growth needs to continue in a progressive Universe. So, don't take these things too personal. Learn how to go within, meditate, and touch the INNER Core of your infinite beauty. You will attract your spiritual partner who is on the same path and energy field to complement and complete your MISSIONS together. And if you remain ALONE to do this, SO BE IT! You are never alone anyways because God is always dwelling within your heart and guiding your life through your soul

Affirmation

" I am grateful and thankful for everything that I have and everything that I am. I am grateful for absolutely NO-THING that is becoming manifested into miracles in every area of my life. I am available and receptive to more good than I can ever imagine possible. I am receptive to more abundance and success, health, wealth, happiness, love, joy, kindness, compassion, plentitude, harmonizing prosperity, healing, and peace in my life. I live in a friendly universe. My life is divinely guided with the presence of God deep in my heart and through the expansion of my soul."

BE THE TRUTH

If you are stuck in a situation and have no clue what to do, maybe it's time to surrender to the higher order of the universe and let go of being in control of the outcome. This doesn't give you the ticket to 'give up' or in any way push you away from manifesting the solution. This is the time to introspect, meditate, go within, and pull yourself out of the madness of the world. Going within means to detach from the external world of phenomenon and getting in touch with your soul, your authentic Self. The answers and solutions you are looking for are not out there in the world. They are embedded deep within your heart and are being generated through your own consciousness. The more you get in touch with the source within, the more you energetically become aligned, find your balance in life, rise above the lower frequencies that you get bombarded on a daily basis, and submerge below the tidal waves of systemic failures of the society. Pull back from judging yourself and others, don't waste your mental energy. Instead invest in your personal development, health, and find a meaningful purpose in your life. By the way, your purpose is not what you do, it's the internal space of your beingness, of how you do what you do at any moment that activates an intention to create peace, healing, abundance, compassion, happiness, and above all, love.

Affirmation

"I am living, moving, and having my being in peace. All of my needs are met. I come from the energy of over flow. I am available and receptive to more abundance, success, and prosperity than I can imagine possible. I live in a friendly universe, radiating my internal light of joy and kindness to the world. Healing is the order of my day. Love is my absolute purpose in every thought, word, and intentional action that generates from my Soul today."

YIELD ... RETURN ... AND LOVE

Everything originates from the Non-being, the void, the No-thing, including you in this universe and what we call life. The origin of being is non-being and the path you are taking is a return movement back to your beginning. This beginning is the spirit of love you came from and appeared from Nothing into the journey or path you are in right now. Each time you YIELD to this mystery and realize that as a whole being you are part of it, you begin to become more of your authentic Self. Shedding the shell of Ego in the moment through humility, your life becomes a reflection of the presence. It becomes a portal and a platform for the great mystery to paint its masterpiece through you as an artist leaving her signature into eternity. Yield, Return, and Love.

Affirmation

"I am a whole being returning to my origin. I am available for more miracles to show up in every area of my life. I am abundant, healthy, compassionate, and at peace. Prosperity is the order of my day. Healing is my nature. Joy and enthusiasm are the fuel for my actions. Love is my destiny. I allow and yield to the universe in full trust."

FALL IN LOVE

When was the last time that you deeply fell in love with yourself? This is not a selfish statement or in any ways leading you to a sense of separation from others. Rather, it's directing your energy to what is the most important aspect of yourself, your recognition of how truly incredible and unique you are. What tends to happen is that we forget about ourselves and many times we either ignore or suppress our feelings when they need to be expressed. Every morning is a new beginning. A renewal of an eternal contract between your Soul and your physical body to align and have a romantic moment in a quiet space of meditation. This is a unique time to fall back in love with yourself all over again, appreciating your own existence and tapping into your highest qualities to come forth. You may not be feeling it at this very moment, yet there is a part of you that is picking up this vibration and will lead you in ways that you'll come back home to the beautiful temple of your Authentic Self. A heart full of love and a discovery of a whole being. This is where God resides in YOU!

Affirmation

"All of my needs are met. I am living, moving, and having my being in divine Love. I am available to more abundance, healing, and prosperity than I can even imagine. The universe supports and guides me to my incredible destiny."

RIDING THE WAVES

When a wave of sadness penetrates your heart and you feel hit by it, you realize your vulnerability in places deep within yourself that require healing. These emotional waves are residues of past experiences and thought patterns that for some reason have formed condensed energy fields inside and need to be cleared from your space. They even create physical symptoms, showing up as fatigue, muscle ache, having a heavy chest, clenching in the upper shoulders, and not seeing clear with an obscure thought patterns. You know what I'm talking about? I think we all go through it in one way or another, getting caught up at times. Remember that this is a transitional state of being which is not in alignment with your Soul's purpose yet it is a gift from your higher Self to re-direct and guide you into areas of yourself that needs healing, that need your self love, self approval, and forgiveness. As you go through this journey we call life, you'll hit these waves and rough seas. Your way of passing through is riding these tides and opening up your heart to give and receive love. To listen to your body, rest, hydrate, and exchange words with a highly conscious individual who does not judge you for what you are experiencing, rather recognizes you for who you truly are.

Affirmation

"I am whole, perfect, and complete. I am living, moving, and having my being in abundance. I am available and receptive to more good than I can imagine in my life. In gratitude, I take my next breath and ride the waves of success, healing, joy, peace, and bliss."

THE GLORY

This very moment is a pause in eternity. As you are reading this, you are becoming the CAUSE onto your own life, becoming more aware of your higher self by just remaining in this space for these brief moments. I just came out from a very deep meditation. Feeling my physical body dissolving in a beautiful light. Beyond the star formations, I felt spacious. As I inhaled, I felt the path of oxygen in the deepest part of my brain, expanding into trillions of cells residing there. It's very challenging to describe this here, yet I'm in a space right now where I intend to share this and rise your vibration because I've already connected to your consciousness and soul. In this field of unity, I've intended a life of joy, prosperity, health, well being, success, love, compassion, beauty, and peace for you already because these qualities were what I was feeling in the fiber of my cells a few moments ago. There are so many people who read my updates that I don't even know of. Then I get a random feedback from a lady with stage 4 cancer, people who are going through such difficult times, and they are being inspired to move on, live in the moment, and overcome whatever challenge they are facing. I become so humbled and touched when I receive these feedbacks, owing it all to a commitment I've made years ago to change the world for the better. The resonance of spiritual practice and meditation, the vibration it exudes to the planet is beyond our understanding and perception. So, in this moment, I'm grateful for the energy that's being transferred to your higher self, and knowing that this loving source is invisible yet indivisible from our HEART and SOUL. It breaths and lives as us in our thoughts, words, actions, and intentions. I solute the Divine in you as the Divine in me is bowing to yours!

KEY TO HAPPINESS

You have an incredible power to shift your perception and change your state of being in a moment. The key to HAPPINESS is to stop pleasure seeking from the materialistic world and aligning yourself with the universal flow of life. When you get caught in chaos, practice contemplating this exercise. Say to yourself: "I am not my physical body, I am not my emotions, I am not my thoughts, and I am not my current circumstances. If I am not these factors, then WHO AM I?" Allow a deeper sense of your wisdom and knowing answer this question. Take some alone time to write whatever comes through you. This is a great way to clear out negative energy you pick up from your situations and other people around who are not aligned with spiritual Truth. After you are done, focus on the energy of gratitude and appreciation. Gratitude is the bridge between your loving soul and internal state of bliss.

Affirmation

"I am available and receptive to more prosperity than I've ever imagined, experienced, or manifested. I am whole, perfect, and complete. I live with purpose and breath with passion in every moment of my life. I am grateful and appreciative for absolutely nothing that manifests into miracles in every area of my life."

MY CHALLENGES

I go through my own struggles on a daily basis. Challenging with deep seeded issues from the past that show up on the surface when my mind gets caught up in the lower energies around me. Sometimes without realizing it, I don't see clearly and get emotionally sucked into these thoughts. However, the only thing I can count on is my commitment and persistence to a vision I hold. As the external circumstances pass through my awareness, I rely on getting pulled through the rough tides with my faith and an inner knowing that "This too Shall Pass". That I have the ability to respond to these changes by directly connecting to my Soul and ask for its guidance. Allowing the obscurities to pass like the clouds in the beautiful sky, like the crashing waves in the hurricane waiting for the sun to break through to calm me down. There is a season for everything and each is governed by a perfect force orchestrating them to their purpose. Allowing the dark seasons to pass through, I remain available and receptive for the eternal power that gives birth to galaxies, beats my heart, and breath through my veins to whisper in my ears and lift me up! I feel it now. I flow into this infinite space with grace and ease.

COMPASSION

What you resist will persist. Had a back-to-back
conversation last night with an old friend of mine who just
recently lost his mom and a mom who just recently lost her
son. The dynamic of loss of a loved one is probably the most
challenging energy field to deal with. It requires the highest
form of compassion and yet a spiritual discernment of
knowing that they will pass through their challenge.
Compassion to me is by far the most sacred spiritual quality
and one that in its purest form, has the strongest effect on
healing. As I was describing affirmations and intention to
one of these individuals and explaining spiritual principles
for self healing, I focused her attention to shift her
perception about life, death, pain, suffering, depression,
hope, purpose, and healing. One thing that has worked for
me personally and most of my clients is shifting the energy
of depression or "I am depressed" to simply: "I have sadness
in me". This is an incredible tool that allows the spirit to
start expressing itself. It will dissolve the tight hold of the
Ego around the heart, loosening it up, and opening it to flow
of self love. Shifting the "I AM" consciousness out of the
lower frequency and acknowledging between what is valid
with what is spiritually invalid thought. I could only see the
light, the beauty, the love, and the compassionate strength
in her aura during our conversation even though she could
not see it in herself. The intensity of pain and suffering
blocks our vision and creates an illusion, a lie that obscures
our perception to Reality. By redirecting the flow of love

and compassion, this obscurity will soon fade. Here is an intention for you if your heart is hurting regardless of what you are growing through in life: "I intend to be healed and be a healing angel to the world"...Start with this. Anytime depression rises up say: "I have sadness within me. I simply experience and feel it pass through me"

Affirmation

"I am living, moving, and having my being in total compassion. Peace is the order of my day. I am whole, perfect, and complete as I was created. I am available to abundance and success, health and wholeness, joy and beauty, love and harmonizing good. I trust and let go. The universe supports me."

HOPE

Here is a healing energy towards humanity. Towards the dis-ease and suffering of the world. To uplift anyone who is going through difficult times and not having their legitimate needs met. As you read this, focus on a grand vision you have for your life. Something that is beyond your imagination. Pick up on a soul quality that you want to manifest more of in the world. Is it love? Is it peace? Is it abundance and prosperity? Is it compassion and harmony? Is it inspiration and enthusiasm? Is it wholeness and well being? Is it creativity and wisdom? or is it all of them? As you continue reading these words coming out of my being from deepest state of meditation right now, realize that I'm holding the space for these qualities to manifest more of in my life and as a united field of consciousness, connected together in this field of oneness, I have you connected as well. There is an intention set in motion right now for us living a life of significance, joy, dignity, and becoming an empty vessel to receive more blessings than we can imagine. To be channels for hope. miracles, and change in our world. YES! it is possible...We are doing it together.

Affirmation

"I am living, moving, and having my being in bliss. Peace is the order of my day. I am available and receptive for more prosperity than I can imagine, experience, or manifest. All of my needs are met. Everything happens for my higher good. I am grateful, thankful, and appreciative for miracles showing up in my life. I release, I let go, I allow, I receive, I share, and I give it all away. The universe supports me."

GET OUT OF DEBT

Un-forgiveness at any level creates a negative energy field in your life that resonates back as 'LACK' to the universe. When you are holding on to un-forgiveness, you are actually sending out a message that: "This person owes me something. This situation did me wrong. There is lack in me." What happens is that the energy you are sending out will translate as 'financial debt' and great 'resistance' to natural flow of abundance in your life. Pain, misery, depression, and anxiety are all functions of holding on to some sort of stagnant, coagulated, rusty energy in your heart and Soul. The nature of life and universe is beauty. The flow of abundance and prosperity comes from your clear space of consciousness where it's resonating from love, compassion, and generosity. The universe responds by corresponding to its own nature when it matches up to higher Soul qualities that are inherent in your heart. So, take a deep breath right now, notice a situation or someone you have not forgiven. Realize that you need to show a bit of courage to do this because it takes guts to break away from mediocrity, from your comfort zone, from your nagging story and victimization. Yes, you need to snap out of it. Haven't you had enough of that miserable story? Aren't you tired of your old BS (belief system)? You have a chance to let go right now. Say: "I forgive and I ask forgiveness from every person, every being, in time and space who is Karmically connected to my present condition". Take another deep breath, hold it, then release by saying the sound of "AHHHHHHHHH"... Today, is going to be a magnificent day. Stay open and receptive to amazing miracles happening in your life

Affirmation

"I forgive and let go, I let go and let God. I am available and receptive to more prosperity, healing, abundance, success, and wealth than I can ever imagine, experience, or manifest. Life flows through me in harmony and peace. All of my needs are met. I am grateful for my existence."

YOU HAVE IT ALL

For the next few seconds that you read this, let go of any anxious thoughts or fear of future you are carrying. Intend this to be a moment of calmness and peace of mind. I invite you to take a deep breath and activate the thought of "I AM GOOD ENOUGH". Being more than your physical body and life experiences, this is a sweet moment to realize your Soulful quality, and eternal being of light and love.

In this very moment, I want you to realize that you are extremely powerful. Do not try to get anything from the world. Happiness and bliss are states of inner being that are inherent within your Soul's character. The world outside has nothing to offer you but bunch of negative news, low conversations around how "everything is messed up". You've seen it and heard it. So many people walk in this fear based mentality. I don't deny the challenges, difficulties, and dis-eases that are so rampant in our society. YES they exist. So does the antidote to all of them. Once you realize that you already have everything you need, BE A DISTRITBUTOR OF LOVE AND JOY. BECOME A PORTAL POINT TO EXPRESS GENEROSITY AND COMPASSION. EXUDE ABUNDANCE in your conversations. If someone says how is life? Get into the feeling tone of excellence! The way out of where you are is to go within your heart and soul. There is no way around it. Don't wait for others to do miracles for you, don't wait for your life to change. Relax into this very second and acknowledge your strength, vigor, intelligence, wisdom, and confidence. If you can not feel this, imagine the best case scenario of your life and go beyond where you are, pulling this energy from your future in to the present moment, the only moment that exists, is here and now.

PERSONAL RELATIONSHIP

So many of us struggle with personal relationships. At one point in your life, you thought you were in love with someone. I don't doubt that. Love is a state of being that is inherent in all of us. It's our natural state of being. On a spiritual journey, your definition of love starts to shift. As you grow and get to know yourself deeper, your tendency to be completely neutral in love expands. Many times, people who are in our lives don't catch up in this evolution. You take on a path of personal discovery and find deeper aspects of yourself, connect with your purpose in life, and become in tune on a vibration that is completely off tune with your partner's. If there is no spiritual partnership, growth, deep connection, support, and an aligned vision together, the relationship will dissolve and dis-integrate from each other. It will not continue. No one is to blame. This is the nature of our human beingness evolving on our course, meeting different angels in our lives that give us what we need at that specific time period. Pointing the finger of blame and judgment on your X-partner or one to be X soon is an immature way of looking at this phenomena. The message this has for you is to discover avenues for forgiveness, discovering ways to expand and grow, discovering to be more loving and compassionate as ever before, even if it has to do with letting go of what no longer serves you. You can heal your life, your relationships, and other people once you open up to healing yourself and loving yourself first. Have self worth and trust the universal source of love to guide you to your destiny.

Affirmation

"I am living, moving, and having my being in love. I am available and receptive to more prosperity than I've ever imagined, experienced, or manifested. My life is divine. I trust the universe to guide me on my path, pull me towards a vision of healing and changing the world for peace, harmony, compassion, kindness, abundance, success, health, and wholeness. I am totally grateful and thankful for NO-THING that manifest as all the miracles in my life. I am blessed and a blessing to the world."

AMAZING ANT

The other day I was hiking and after meditation I was observing the world around me. Fascinated as I took my steps, I totally became one with all the creatures I was walking by. One of them being ants. I truly love them. These incredible insects. I was walking by them and noticing their persistence, resilience, and discipline as they were roaming around, doing their thing, minding their own business. I was being very careful not to step over any. Do they ever sleep? Do they ever take lunch or dinner break? Do they ever complain about the heavy loads they are moving around? Do they ever dream about being something less or more than being their authentic ant Self? I was wondering about these questions and having my imagination running wild. I literally became one and could see my antennas picking up signals in the traffic jam among my buddies. Every one of us had our own specific purpose. Our purpose was to Be the best Ant we could possibly be. Our purpose was to create more of who we are and more of who we could be in every moment of our existence. As I greeted my friends, the only thing mattered was encouraging each other and helping each other. if one was becoming crushed under a heavy load of a seed, we would naturally help out. We jumped on each other's back, split the seed, and each took part of the whole to lower the burden from the others. We weren't competing with each other. It was a space of perfect cooperation and paying it forward to my fellow Ant buddies. My introspection took me into a world of pure unconditional love. No judgment, no wanting to be something I'm NOT, and an inner awareness of content. Contentment for momentarily being an ant, a simple yet sophisticated being of pure love, courage, and joy. Lesson learned from this magnificent creature. I told myself I'll write about this experience sometime soon and see what comes out of it. Here it is, if you connected to it, the divine ant in me is honoring the divine ant in you. Namaste.

Affirmation

"I am part of the perfection of our universe. I live a magnificent life of simplicity and pure joy. I am living, moving, and having my being in God. I am available to more prosperity than I can imagine, experience, or manifest than before. God's will for my life releases me and sets me free. Gratitude and appreciation light my path and show me the way. Healing is the order of my day. "

FORM FOLLOWS CONSCIOUSNESS!

Many of us get caught up in our old stories, the past conditions that take us hostage in our present moments and get projected into the future. Realize that FORM follows your CONSCIOUSNESS, or the thoughts that you think moment by moment, and the feelings you maintain with those thoughts (the state of your awareness of the Real) do create your reality. Make it a habit to deliberately use your positive thinking muscles and imagination for the best case scenario of your life in order to raise your vibration.

The universe responds by corresponding to its own unique nature and pattern which is you, your thoughts, and feeling tones. This way you can shift your current paradigm and create New Beginnings. This requires your commitment. Meditating regularly will make this become a great habit.

Affirmation

"I live in integrity and alignment with my higher self. I allow the universal mind of kindness, abundance, compassion, love, peace, creativity, joy, and brilliance to take over my life, feelings, and thoughts."

GRAND PURPOSE

Mystically speaking, you live for a grand PURPOSE which is to reflect and reveal the divine nature and beauty of God. Once you realize that this is a common purpose of human beings, you'll find out that you get to fulfill this purpose through finding your innate gifts, talents, capacities, genius, creativity, and sharing them with the world.

You hold a vision that is greater than yourself, you'll live a life of significance that is not all about you, and you'll find common grounds with other souls traveling through this earth school. Fear of dying and death disappears when you connect to your grand purpose in life and have strong faith that you are an eternal spiritual being taking on a temporary human form to get to express the presence of God's perfection, through you, as you, as your thoughts, as your actions, AS YOUR LIFE...The spirit knows why you are here, your soul knows where you are going. Surrender yourself to it, yield to your power within, and make a mighty difference in this time during our human species evolution!...These are the time for spiritual warriors stepping up to the game for manifesting global just society, cooperation, kindness, compassion, abundance, love, and above all PEACE ON OUR PLANET TODAY! ARE YOU UP FOR THIS MISSION?

LET GO AND LET GOD

There is higher order to the divine beauty of universal mind. When you release your attachments to any outcome, surrender into the energy that created you, and trust that your life is being guided just as you were guided as an embryo into becoming a human infant, you become liberated and free. Your heart fills with unlimited love, compassion, and joy. You'll smile for absolutely no reason! Just because you exist is enough reason to celebrate. It's time to let it GO, and let God take over every breath.

Affirmation

"I let go and let God handle every aspect of my life. I trust the universal mind to guide me and open up doors, create possibilities, and manifest all the blessings in my life."

LOVE HEALS

When you lose a precious someone close to you, you literally feel loss of power through your heart center. What we experience as heart break is a loss of this energy directly from our heart Chakra. Remember that the loss is a temporary illusion of the physical form. In essence, there's never a loss of anything because there's only one life that everything lives and breathes through in eternity. You must realize that your power is embedded in the energy of LOVE. That's where the replacement comes from. When you decide that you rise above your heart ache, experience it, and then open your heart to unlimited LOVE that's available everywhere, you will shine. This is where healing happens. This is where your completion with your experience takes place.

As you invite more of this energy in your heart, you'll have more of it to give away. It becomes an avalanche of everlasting good, of pure energy that not only heals you, but heals the entire world. Oh, I'm feeling that love right now, and I'm transmitting it through my heart and my soul directly to your heart and your soul.

OPEN DOORS

You are continuously unfolding on your Soul's journey one day at a time, one moment at a time. There is always a new beginning, a new set point, as each time you connect to your inner being and recognize your authentic power. Doors will open when you contemplate your relationship with oneness and stay in gratitude for everything that's going on, while you set your intentions in accordance to, and balance with, the laws of Universe. Keep on dancing forward.

Affirmation

"I am living, moving, and having my being in love, in God, in abundance, and in complete health. Every experience opens new doors in my life by the knowing that universal laws support my life to reach my destiny. Oh, I HAVE A MAGNIFICENT DESTINY."

YOUR SOUL'S VISION

There is a perfect vision for your life at Soul level. The way to connect with your purpose and destiny is to go within, silent your mind, meditate, and align yourself with life's vision for you. When you make yourself receptive and available, the universe reveals its own expression through you, as you, as your life. Miracles show up because they are already here and you are becoming present to them for expression!

... Are you available?

Affirmation

"I am available, I am receptive, and I am open to receive the great miracles of life. Bring it on baby."

SELF REFLECTION

How often do you take the time to look deep within your soul and release those personalities that don't serve your higher good? Sometimes it's necessary to let go of what we so dearly hold on to, and to open ourselves up to new discoveries, to make ourselves available for our soul's evolution. It's not difficult. It just requires an intention of doing it. I invite you to take some time today and self reflect with an open heart, asking yourself this question:

"What is the authentic purpose of my soul?"

FLY UP HIGH

Comparing yourself to others is one of the toughest feelings to deal with. It happens to all of us because we lose touch with our own inner strengths, capabilities, and blessings. I'm a big fan of GRATITUDE because bringing your attention deliberately on things you are appreciative of, brings you into the present moment. It will give you a sense of grace.

Grace and Gratitude are twins who share lots of love together. Follow one, the other will appear out of nowhere and lift your spirit like mighty eagle flying in open skies. Go for it, I'm serious, enough of looking down at yourself thinking that another person is better than you. I invite you to say "I'm GRATEFUL" as many times as you can today, silently to yourself. Observe the world around you change instantly when you do this.

"I am grateful for being able to walk with grace, hold my head up, open my heart, attract abundance in my life, radiate love, and walk in peace. There is so much I'm grateful for."

LOOKING WITHIN

I've learned that everyone is traveling through this journey we call life in order to learn multiple lessons so that they can evolve and spiritually grow. I realize that the more I release any attachments and allow people I love to BE themselves, the more I'm helping them and lifting their spirit. Stop controlling others and casting your own fears, doubts, worries on them. That's a cheap shot!

I invite you to take a deep look within yourself, your thoughts, your actions, your feelings, and your intentions. YES, it's kind of scary if you've been running away from yourself. Have the COURAGE!

Transformation and healing starts with cleaning up our own mess first. I keep reminding myself about this on a consistent basis in order to keep myself connected and aware. The more I meditate, the more I can feel the distinction between my mind driven Ego and my soul. It's so easy to fall off the path though, especially when you get so emotional and see the people around you going through their life's challenges. Compassion is a key factor. Love and compassion can diffuse those hidden feelings that come up and try to snatch your awareness. Try it! The next time your irritation surface up, remind yourself that you are a compassionate, loving being.

You are not your experiences, or the experiences you are being caught up with other people. Yes, it happens, you fall off. What's next? What do you do next?

NO BLAME, NO SHAME

Are you going to go into blame and shame, guilt, pulling fingers, or are you going to grow from this process? See, life will test you to your limits until you learn the lessons you are here to experience and learn in order for your soul to take its next stage into its evolutionary consciousness. That's why you are here to do.

Anything else is an illusion of the Ego ... Take responsibility for it and help all of us clean up our polluted minds. The collective human consciousness right now needs us to be aware and sensitive to our own mental dramas. We can't add any more to what already is ... Just watch the evening news and you know what I'm talking about.

So, I'm all in ... ARE YOU?... WILL YOU?

As I'm writing this I'm holding the reader, YOU, in high vibration of love and compassion. I know you are growing through many challenges, issues, and problems. Why I know that, because I'm experiencing the same ... I have all the problems you have in my own little world. However, I know one thing. I know that by raising my vibration and consciousness, not only I'm helping myself, but I'm helping you and everyone else you are connected to.

See, we are all connected to someone and that someone is connected to someone else. Ultimately, we are all connected and mirror images of each other. So, let's do this ... I hope this message finds you and shifts you in a positive way ... gives you a lift, a boost in energy, inspires you to take constructive and positive actions for yourself first, then for people you love, then for strangers! *I love you.*

BE AWESOMENESS!!!

Talking about spirituality and reading books is pretty cool. It's hype! People will pick up a sense of feeling GOOD temporarily and look for a quick fix to their problems.

Practicing it is awesome though because you become true reflection of your inner world, thoughts, and feelings without judgment. You tap into love energy that's around you all the time. You flow with nature, and you radiate peace that surpasses human understanding. Are you up for the practice?

Affirmation

"I am living, moving, and having my being in ONENESS with God. My life is the reflection of the only ONE life. The universe supports me. I am available for success, health, and abundance now. Come what may."

EMPOWERED!!!

As you read this I invite you to feel empowered, I invite you to feel your uniqueness, your gifts, talents, capabilities, and all the blessings that are residing within you. I invite you to step out from what the society has labeled you and just for these brief seconds step away from your problems. Look at them from a distance. Connect to your inner power, purity, light, and strength that are shining directly from your heart. Connect to the life force, the infinite universal energy that's running through your body with each breath.
YOU ARE A MAGNIFICENT BEING, YOU ARE ETERNAL, YOU ARE LOVE ITSELF.

Allow these words to penetrate your soul and Re-read this as often today as you can with an intention to rise above your challenges and turn your life around for the better. You can do it; you have a mandate to do it.

Affirmation

"Today, I pay attention to what my heart desires, I step away from the masks I've put on my face and become REAL, Become my true self."

OWN IT!

If you feel a sense of heaviness in your shoulders, chest, and upper stomach areas, you may be carrying other people's energies of guilt, doubt, worry and resentment. These feelings slowly eat through your mental and physical body. Like a parasite sucking out the living life out of you and potentially becoming cancer.

Solution: Spiritual discernment, self realization, DEEP FORGIVENESS work, meditation, and taking care of yourself through exercise with high quality nutrition. Dis-ease is self inflicted, so is its counterpart: VITALITY. It's time to wake up and live a happy, healthy, free life!

Affirmation

"I am living a FREE life. Opening my heart, shining my light, giving more than taking, sharing more than hording, allowing the natural energies of love, joy, kindness, peace, abundance, compassion, and gratitude shower my entire being with molecules of vitality gushing through my blood stream in every moment of my life."

PEACE & LOVE

"Peace is not the absence of violence. Peace is the dynamic of harmonizing good."

- Michael Bernard Beckwith

Focus your attention and intention on all the great things that are happening around the globe. You won't hear that act of kindness, compassion, sharing, and love on the news. You want to stand for peace rather than eliminating hate, war, or crime. You want to stand for love, rather than getting caught up in fear, doubt, and worry. Keep love and peace the focal point of your attention and intention. Allow your consciousness guide you through your path.

COM-PASSION

You can conquer anyone's heart through 'Compassion' which means Com=*with* and Passion=*deep* feeling. Rising above any ordain thinking is accomplished through being compassionate and loving, deeply feeling yourself and others, recognizing the divine within them as one and the same with the divine within you. At that instant moment, you have reached the mountain top of your TRUTH. Today, let's be more compassionate, more loving, more caring, and more ourselves for we are the only one that can truly CHANGE the WORLD.

Affirmation

"I am living, moving, and having my being in Divine love, compassion, caring, abundance, success, healing, and peace, armed with my TRUTH and my heart wide open, I stand for the CHANGE I WANT TO SEE IN THE WORLD".

THOUGHTS MATTER

What do you think of your life? The way you describe your experience will eventually create more of the same experience. As you center yourself and meditate, you bring harmony into your life. Your connection to the universe is the key to resolve the challenges you are facing. Change your thoughts about who you are, what you are, where you are, and why you are here on this planet. As a result, your life will CHANGE. Open your heart, trust, and allow.

Affirmation

"I am open and receptive to more good than I can ever imagine. I allow life to direct me to my destiny. I trust in the power that created me, that loves me, and that knows the answers to my prayers."

LUMINOSITY

Do you find yourself asking the deeper questions about life and existence more often? Or perhaps waking up from a dream like state and realize that there is more to what you can physically experience? These are signs of spiritual awakening.

The thoughts that guide you towards higher state of consciousness and the feelings that connect you to everyone are your soul communicating with you. Boundaries and separation dissolve. A sense of immense peace and unconditional love takes over your entire being. Am I speaking to you? If so, you are becoming aware of your true state of luminosity; a BEING of pure LIGHT, timeless, space less being who resides in infinite state of pure bliss. Connected to your purpose in life, armed with courage and compassion, you find yourself manifesting and co-creating your divine destiny knowing that the universe is handling everything for you. Am I talking to you? I know who YOU ARE.

Affirmation

"I am pure love. Life supports me through all of my challenges. I open my heart and bow down to the infinite beauty of the entire cosmos."

YOUR BIRTH CERTIFICATE

Love and happiness are not age dependent, circumstance dependent, financial dependent, nor have anything to do with your social economic status. They are states of your inner BEING. When you touch someone's heart, you create happiness in them. When you are free of your Ego driven mind, you open up to love. When you give and share, you reside in both love and happiness. BE them, practice them, and you attract more of them as you become more of YOUR AUTHENTIC self. Search for them outside, and the illusion of the materialistic world will blind you. As you meditate more often, you will realize that YOU ARE "LOVE" ITSELF. No separation. Your birth certificate will say:

Description: A beautiful Child of the Universe
First Name: LOVE
Last Name: HAPPINESS
Birth Date: INFINITY
Place of Birth: ETERNITY OF THE COSMOS

Affirmation

"I am living, moving, and having my being in LOVE and HAPPINESS. The universe supports me with infinite abundance and success, healing and health, wealth and prosperity into my life...and so it is...amen"

WHAT DO YOU SEE?

When you look into the eyes of another human being, notice the vastness of their soul rather than judging them based on their race, religion, color, or their nationality. Become aware of these social conditions and truly step out of telling yourself made up stories. As you connect to your inner divine nature and embrace your higher BEING through meditation, what will happen is you'll start connecting to the divine nature of others. You'll notice that everyone is part of this unlimited, infinite energy. Everyone is divine, not just people, but every animal, tree, mineral, and creature that co-exist with you on this planet. This is the level of consciousness that heals the world and is glowing through the shining light of the spirit. This is who you and I are if we just wake up to it and get out of our own way. Namaste

---

Affirmation

"I am open and receptive to more good, more miracles, and more love in my life than I can even imagine. I welcome the UNKNOWN."

DESTINATION

What makes you present to the journey is the process of
your soul's awakening to its authentic BEING. What do I
mean by that? Your soul is unfolding in your human
paradigm and you are connecting to the universe's vision
for you which is already here and always have been through
eternity. The process of waking up from the dream of
human drama re-connects you to your soul's destiny. Take a
deep breath my friend, IT'S ALL GOOD! ENJOY YOUR VERY
NEXT BREATH BECAUSE THAT'S WHERE THE MYSTERY OF
ALL LIFE IS; IT'S RIGHT WITHIN EACH BREATH.

Affirmation

*"I am living, moving, and having my being in waking up to
my authentic self. My SOUL IS BLISSFUL AND REALLY
PEACEFUL."*

TOUCHING DIVINITY

Here's a glimpse at divinity. I just meditated and my breathing is very deep. My mind is completely at peace, very quiet. The only thing I hear is sounds of the birds singing outside from my window and the crickets orchestrating their symphony. It's such an awe aspiring space. I feel my heart beat. I can follow the stream flow of my blood in the smallest vessels of my body. I can see them opening up, extracting oxygen and nutrients to every cell. I can picture my DNA molecules dancing to the music of my soul's song, the vibration of life passing through the infinite space of my physical body. I feel the stillness, the joy, the overflow of love that is waiting to be expressed from my actions. My interest is on divine consciousness. I'm connected to the infinite life of God. From this space of oneness, I'm sending you blessings and prayers of healing, prosperity, abundance, peace, order, harmony, everything that your heart desires, perfect health, and laughter.

Affirmation

"I am one with ONENESS, life supports me in everything I set my intention to. Today I intend to love, to heal, to inspire, and to be abundantly wealthy for myself and others in order to raise the collective consciousness."

BE, FEEL & MOVE LIKE WATER

I invite you to take a deep breath as you are reading this and allow the softness of the energy of what is to follow to go within your entire being.

Picture yourself as 'WATER' going down the stream, so effortless and smooth. Imagine places in your life where you are having challenges. Now, as you take a deep breath, imagine this flowing stream of water, softly and gently penetrating the areas of your concern. Imagine the qualities of water washing away your fears, worries, and anxieties. Yield to this powerful element which you are composed of. We are 75-80% made up of water. It nourishes our cells, gives life to our planet, and is the most powerful force that exists. Be flexible in your approach to life, just like water is. It can be found as vapor, liquid, or solid, yet it is just WATER in all stages.

YOU ARE A SPIRITUAL BEING HAVING A TEMPORARY HUMAN INCARNATION. Feel that in your heart and bring that aspect of your beingness into your daily life. As you read and -re-read this, send out a PRAYER OF LOVE, PEACE, HARMONY, and HEALING TO EVERYONE ON OUR PLANET! INCLUDE ANY BEING THAT IS DEPENDENT ON WATER AND IS MADE UP OF WATER.

Affirmation

"I am living, moving, and having my being in complete peace and harmony. My life is filled with joy, my heart is filled with love, and I'm always able to yield to my greatness. Overflow with pure compassion, I GIVE IT ALL AWAY NOW".

INSTRUMENT OF PEACE

How can you be an instrument of peace? As you read this, take a deep breath, you might have to read this over and over because each time you'll feel more inner peace, you'll feel your heart rate slowing down, and you'll feel yourself more connected. I'm connected right now, sending you an amazing energy of love, coming down from the top of your head as a beautiful white light, shining down to your neck, heart, vertebral column, inside your spine, passing through the entire muscles of your lower body and out to your feet.

Take another deep breath, visualize your life in this exact moment as whole, perfect, and complete. With that breath you just took, your needs were completely met, calmness was the only thing your heart was feeding on. Love is the only energy that is circulating in your blood stream with each heart beat and nourishing your cells right now. Imagine your physical, emotional, and Soul body lining up in divine order and complete harmony with the universal one life. That life is YOU, is all in YOU. Welcome to YOUR AUTHENTIC SELF.

EN-JOY

I'm excited for another new day, a chance for an awesome beginning. If you notice, you are always beginning at some new point. You are here and now, in the moment, over and over, but it's always fresh. You have a choice to reflect back in your heart and give it your best. Enjoy the moment as you live your life with purpose, passion, compassion, enthusiasm, inspiration, and immense love. Every beginning is decided by you and YOU only. BE PRESENT and EN-JOY

Affirmation

"I am living, moving, and having my being in the MOMENT, in LOVE".

POWER OF INTENTION

The power of intention is a magical energy to tap into. It's the essence of all being, it's what beats your heart and automatically makes you breath. It's the oxygen that supplies your blood stream to make your cells function; it's the feeling behind all the joy, peace, compassion, and kindness.

Intention is beyond the creation. It's space less, yet it's everywhere and its circumference is nowhere. It has no beginning, no end. It's beautiful yet shapeless, abundant and endless. The more you think about describing it, the farther you get from feeling it because it reveals itself through your heart. Go deep within, meditate, and you'll find out that intention is YOU!

Affirmation

"I INTEND to love, to heal, to inspire, and to be abundant for myself and others in order to raise the collective cosmic consciousness, and so it is , Amen."

HEAVEN ON EARTH

Opening yourself up and becoming vulnerable by emotionally connecting to your inner child is a MUST in order for transformation to take place.

We sometimes hide behind our smiles, vocations, family responsibilities, excessive food intake, hanging with friends, sex, or making money. Yet, we forget the most important aspect to our lives, which is SELF LOVE. We cannot grow unless we are willing to pay the price of loving ourselves, caring, and shining a compassionate light to our inner BEING first. This is the task of a spiritual warrior, one who is willing to be authentic, real, and accepting himself without fear of judgment. Yes, WE ARE ALL SPIRITUAL WARRIORS.

World peace is a reflection of our inner peace. When enough of us find inner peace, we'll create what's been dreamed already in the mind of God: HEAVEN on EARTH!

Affirmation

"I am so grateful and thankful for being connected to my inner child, loving, caring, embracing, and accepting him for all he IS. I AM, GOD IS".

INNER SPACE

I had one of my most intense and emotional group meditations last night. As I was going on my journey, I got to a point where I had every soul present with me form a chain around our planet by holding each other's hand. Then we visualized the entire planet being showered by a beautiful white/Gold color. These included all of YOU, all the animals, plants, minerals, oceans, mountains, and everything you can imagine into prayer of healing, love, abundance, joy, prosperity, and peace. I then specifically included the Orphan kids we visited on Sunday and had them in highest level of consciousness. I don't quite cry during meditation, but this time I did. To be honest with you, I'm so humbled and in dis-belief that I get to be a vortex for accomplishing this. I'm humbled to have my dream from childhood manifested as I'm doing: *To be an agent for meditation and healing.* Who would have thought I'd find my path this way. I don't have words to describe what I felt last night. Gratitude with immense unconditional love is the closest I can get. Today is the best day you'll ever have. Remember, IT'S ALL GOOD.

Affirmation

"I am love in action. I am available and receptive to more good than I can ever imagine. I live a purposeful life with full abundance, success, and passion."

HEALING YOUR HEART

I would like to paint a beautiful picture for those of us who have witnessed transformation of someone so special and dear to us from our physical world into the world of spirit. I invite you to take a deep breath as you are reading this:

While you are contemplating their memory, I invite you to pick an occasion when you felt complete ONENESS with them. As you embrace them in your arm and imagine their smell, touch, look, and how they sound like, I invite you to feel their BEING inside the breath you just took. Imagine the oxygen molecules that are feeding your entire body, are essence of your loved one. Imagine the energy going through your cells, inside your DNA, wrapped around by your loved one through eternity and captured in this instance, sending you a message of love, patience, healing, compassion, joy, and peace that passes human understanding. They are right within your heart and the healing energy I'm sending you is matching their healing energy to strengthen your SOUL. Breathe out, relax, ALL IS WELL.

Affirmation

"I am living, moving, and having my being in abundance and success, health and healing, inspiration and enthusiasm. I cherish the memories of my loved one and embrace their LOVE to honor their SOUL."

SINCERITY

There is something very magical about the earliest moments in the morning. Like right now, I feel so calm and my creativity is at its peak. Feeling so grateful for where the spirit of love is taking my life. How the universe is orchestrating the little details to unfold my destiny. It's pretty incredible when you surrender to your higher self and allow life to carry you through. I'm excited for what's coming. Even though I have no clue what's coming. I am open and receptive to more good in my life than I can ever imagine. I sincerely have this prayer for you also.

I send you this blessing to have your heart open, your souls inspired with passion! I see you prosperous, wealthy, healthy, abundant, divinely guided, and peaceful. I see you soaring and spiritually uplifted, happy and constantly joyous, beautiful and absolutely free with your desires met already. Namaste.

Affirmation

"I am living, moving, and having my BEING in love and compassion. Today is the BEST day of my life with all of my NEEDS met. I accept what's best for my highest evolution and gratefully call it forth in my life."

HAVE THE COURAGE

Have the COURAGE to step out of your current circumstances that chain you down in lower energies of pain, depression, fear, anxiety, and shame. It all starts with a thought in your mind and dreaming your freedom to BE YOURSELF into reality. You are more powerful than you think you are. The entire cosmos conspired you into this existence. Your body is made from the elements of the stars. You are made up of water, oxygen, carbon, and billions of astral molecules into this magnificent conscious BEING. Giving in to people's idea of you, what they think you should be, or having anyone CONTROLLING you is un-acceptable.

You are love in manifestation with each breath. Do you get what I'm saying? I don't really care who you programmed to think you are and what your relationship is to me! BUT I do care at what level of AWARENESS you are operating from because my entire mission in life is to WAKE YOU UP TO YOUR MAJESTIC, REAL SELF!!! WAKE UP BABY, WAKE UP!!!

Affirmation

"I am living, moving, and having my being in complete AWARENESS of my authentic self. I live for myself knowing that divine love of universe guides me in every step of my life."

THE ART OF CRYING

There is a magical mystery in the art of crying. Your true identity is not the emotions, feelings, and any pain that is passing through your emotional body. Be aware of not identifying yourself with what the mind and physical body is experiencing. Your awareness of being the experience that is experiencing allows you to witness yourself pass through all the turmoil while you are anchored in the realm of the spirit. As your emotions flow through, your body cleanses; heart opens up, and your entire nervous system relaxes. After you relax through the experience, your body becomes numb, your chest feels light, and the tightening in your shoulder muscles and neck loosen up. There is a subtle euphoria that follows this process. It's just a very sacred atmosphere. I don't know if anyone reading this has had the similar experience from this point of view. If not, keep on meditating until you get here...
Namaste.

Affirmation

"I am living, moving, and having my being in peace and harmony. I let go and let God handle every movement in my life. My destiny is a great destiny. All is well. "

THE HEART'S STRUGGLES

Do you ever find yourself caught in the battle between the HEART and the MIND? Where one tells you something and the other something else? What do you do? I allow my heart to expand around what it's yearning to express. I open my heart so whatever action comes from it is expressed through pure love. My mind, however, wonders how I get that done! The creative genius of my mind becomes the perfect vehicle to direct and guide my heart's unlimited passion. So, a balance is created between the heart and the mind. The key to it for me is: MEDITATION

Affirmation

"I am worthy of my heart's desires and the truth of my mind harmonizing my actions into divine manifestations".

I AM GRATEFUL TO BE!

Let me ask you this: Is your Soul on Fire? Do you have a burning desire in the morning to wake up and unleash the power within you? Are you living in the moment and give it all you have for just TODAY. making it the best day in your life? I feel like you are searching for an answer. I feel like you've been contemplating these questions long enough to be open and receptive to this message you are reading. I feel like all you need is a bit of faith, a little bit of inspiration, and a helping hand to guide you on your path. If you are that person ready and available to AWAKEN, I'm talking to you!

Some may read this post and the energy behind it may go right over their head. (That's fine). However, I'm speaking to your over-SOUL. I'm speaking to that intuition deep within your heart to AWAKEN...Let the burning desire reveal itself. Let yourself be authentic and powerful, joyous and grateful, passionate and cheerful, Creative and absolutely beautiful. LET YOURSELF BE YOU. LET IT.

Affirmation

"I am giving myself permission to be ME. I am connected and grateful to be the Real me. All is WELL."

FLOW WITH CHANGE

Here is something I invite you to realize. The only certainty in life is 'change'. When you truly understand this and release yourself from the 'fear of unknown', your life takes on a peaceful vibration. You are not constantly under threat of 'what is going to happen?'. You inherently know and accept 'change' as a natural phenomenon. Open your heart to this and release yourself from the burden of always 'BEING in CONTROL'.

The universe is in 'FLOW' and changing every second as it expands. You also as a Spiritual being having a temporary human incarnation are on a voyage into constant change. Allow life to carry you through by being flexible, adoptable, and teachable. Trust and have faith.

Affirmation

"I am open and receptive to more good than I can ever imagine. I allow changes in life to carry me to my destiny. I trust the universe and my soul to guide me, support me, nourish me, and protect me in my journey. Life is deliciously WONDERFUL."

RETURNING TO AUTHENTICITY

I fell for my Ego's expectation of wanting something in return, or a payback, or fulfilling an inner need from an individual. As I was speaking, my conversation took the tonality of defensiveness. The interesting part is that I became aware of entering the lower, negative energy of the person I was speaking to right away; however, I could not maneuver myself out of the drag. When you have turmoil within yourself, it's a perfect fertile land for your Ego to strengthen itself and push you out of integrity with your Soul. One of the Ego's major needs is 'trying to prove your point'. This can waste a lot of good energy from you and the other person in any relationship. Through my awareness, I went back to my strong friendship bridge, a mutual love between us, expressing my sentiments, and learning from my experience. I also re-connected back to our mutual intentions. Lesson learned.

Affirmation

"I am living, moving, and having my being in strong faith. I know my life is supported by the good of the universe."

RISE UP

What can you do to RAISE your vibration and soul energy in order to attract and co-create that which is your divine destiny? Yes, you can do that. Every hour by the hour, take a deep breath and detach yourself from the world of circumstances, the hurried life, the rampaged thoughts, arguments, freeways, anxieties, fear, and worries. Take few moments each hour and experience your deeper connection to the universe. Experience your oneness. Two things you must do regularly:

One, FORGIVE yourself and everyone who has ever come into your experience for everything said and done knowingly or unknowingly at any level of consciousness.

Second, focus on the SOULUTIONS in your life, focus on the best case scenarios in your life, and anticipate them in advance.

Come from faith and a deep knowing that the universe provides that we live in a friendly, supportive, loving universe, that ALL OF YOUR NEEDS ARE MET, even now as you are reading this. Its 5:30 AM FOR ME. I HAVE YOU IN HIGHEST SPACE OF LOVING COMPASSION, SENDING YOU PRAYERS OF ABUNDANCE AND SUCCESS, HOLDING YOU IN TOTAL HEALTH, HEALING, PEACE, AND HARMONY. That you can count on!

Affirmation

"I am living, moving, and having my being in Peace. All of my needs are met at every level of my existence. I am open and receptive to more miracles, more good, more abundance, more success, more health, more divine loving relationships, and more joy than I can ever imagine possible. Come what may."

ONE LIFE

In this exact moment as I'm writing this, so many scenarios are happening in people's lives all around the world. Every one of us is going through challenges, some really hard ones, some not as difficult. Yet, we are all experiencing life from our point of view, from our own prism. The only thing I'm in tune with right now though is my breath. I'm consciously breathing as I invite you to do RIGHT NOW as well, and I feel my heart beat. Its beating slowly, kind of synchronized with my breath. Now, imagine my breath and heart beat connected to yours as one field of consciousness. Then, expand this awareness to everyone in your family, friends, and around the globe. Take a deep breath, hold it, Pray for health, wealth, happiness, peace, love, joy, abundance, kindness, creativity, compassion, and more love than you can imagine possible for everyone. Release your breath slowly, smile, and carry this vibrant energy knowing that you just uplifted the entire consciousness of the universe. FEELS GREAT RIGHT? Namaste.

Affirmation

"I am one with the universe. My life is the life of God. I am supported, loved, and blessed in my life and pass that energy to everyone freely. I am open and receptive to more abundance than I can ever imagine."

YOUR WORD MAKES
YOUR WORLD

I always talk about the POWER OF OUR WORDS. It's so easy to break apart somebody's WORLD with your WORD. Be conscious and aware of what comes out of your mouth.

We are conduits of love, generosity, peace, compassion, and kindness using our words. However, we can also become an agent of hate, destruction, negativity, and pain.

THE CHOICE IS YOURS!

(Notice that between world and word there is an L missing. That L stands for LOVE. KEEP ON SAYING LOVING WORDS TO EVERYONE.)

Affirmation

"I am an agent of peace. With my heart full of love, I choose to use my words into creating a LOVING world for everyone, including myself first".

CONTEXT

So many times we get hurt and hurt our loved ones just by lack of communication and misunderstanding. In a healthy relationship, what matters most is the integrity of your friendship and the bond you have already established with others. YOUR WORDS MEAN A LOT! Everyone goes through a hard time; people go through emotional roller coasters. If you deeply care for your partner or whom you call 'FRIEND', don't attack their integrity, character, or intentions. You may have taken the entire story you've experienced out of context from what really happened. Sometimes, we are the ones who are playing a blame game to get away from our own insecurities. I believe love and forgiveness are attributes that can heal the situation.

> ### Affirmation
>
> *"I am love, I have love. I am forgiving, I forgive. I am abundant, I have abundance and prosperity. Life supports me."*

I AM WHOLE, PERFECT, AND COMPLETE

One of my most favorite affirmations that I always say is :

> *"I am whole , perfect, and complete as I was created. I belong."*

This thought aligns you to your original perfection as a spiritual being having a temporary human incarnation. It closes the gap between the senses of separation and raises your healing capacity to match the universal ALL GOOD OF GOD. For me, it always does wonders. In my challenging times, it calms me down, re-connects me to the Source of my Being. It soothes my heart when it is hurting. I believe in it. I have faith that I AM WHOLE, PERFECT, AND COMPLETE. I DO BELONG IN THE COSMOS JUST BECAUSE I EXIST; IT'S MY INHERENT RIGHT TO BE JOYOUS! THERE IS NOTHING LACKING OR MISSING IN ME. THE WORLD OF ILLUSION HAS NO EFFECT ON MY STRONG FAITH.

Please keep this affirmation on you and repeat it frequently with conviction.

ARE YOU ON YOUR OWN SIDE?

Here's a beautiful concept for spiritual practice: WHEN YOU ARE MET WITH CHALLENGES, LIFE IS GIVING YOU ENOUGH RESISTANCE TO BREAK UP YOUR COMFORT ZONE AND PRETTY MUCH KICKING YOUR BUTT, "ARE YOU ON YOUR OWN SIDE?" Meaning that so often we try to get support from outside, or perhaps we try to be "THERE" for others and play their Jesus Christ savior role, but we forget ourselves! WE DON'T GIVE OURSELVES LOVE, ATTENTION, CARE, KINDNESS, OR WORD OF ENCOURAGEMENT.

So, let me ask you again: Are you on your own side? Or you are running away from yourself, bringing up excuses all the time to eat well, exercise regularly, meditate, do act of kindness in service to others, and educate yourself, Being kind to yourself. This is the KICK YOUR ASS WAKE UP CALL POST. It's honestly for me, to remind me to be on my own side on a moment by moment basis in order to bring out the best in me so that I can shine my love and light out to the world without any inhibition. Are you on your own side now?

Affirmation

"I yield to the presence of life. I give up my arguments about outside circumstances and open myself to availability. I release my judgments of myself and start BEING ON MY OWN SIDE, MY OWN ALLY, and WITH COMPLETE RESPECT AND JOY."

CALMING THE STORM

Don't allow the storms of your life hold you back on your grand vision. You are bigger than your challenges, stronger than your worries, and more intelligent than anyone who tells you otherwise. Keep your faith SOLID in yourself and be willing to manifest miracles in your life because you are already a miracle in action.

Affirmation

"I allow complete peace and abundance flourish into my life. Divine healing is the order of my day."

CHERISH THEM!

There is nothing like loving someone so deeply and unconditionally. Once you are at that space, you don't see separation anymore. The individual which means 'un-divided', literally feels like and becomes like 'ONE' being. This happens at our soul level.

There are people in your life that appear out of nowhere and all of the sudden you know you've known them forever. You know they've played a major role in your other lives. Cherish these angels who show up in your life. They've traveled light years, and many lifetimes to meet up with you again. If you know a person like that, you know what I'm talking about. I'm sending my love to all the loving soul's out there who are completing their sacred missions.

Affirmation

"I am available and receptive to more LOVE than I can ever imagine. Life supports me. Abundance is the calling of my Day. Healing reigns supreme. I am blessed".

HEALING YOUR SOUL

The healing of the body and the mind only follows after the healing of the Soul. What heals the soul is Love, is being in tune with you at the deepest level, achieved through meditation and prayers. Communing with nature and surrounding yourself with people who are traveling the path with you.

Become aware of your breathing right now. YES! Right now, inhale through your nose and hold your breath for couple of seconds. Imagine the best case scenario for your entire day. Say in your mind with deep conviction:

> *"ALL OF MY LEGITIMATE NEEDS ARE MET AT EVERY LEVEL OF MY EXISTENCE."*

Breathe out slowly through your mouth. Repeat this several times. Re-read what I wrote here throughout the day as a reminder of anchoring yourself in the MOMENT as we are traveling through eternity of time.

As you expand your consciousness, you realize we are beyond time, beyond space. We are at the center of the universe with our circumferences BEING in absolutely NOWHERE, but we are NOW-HERE! Your point of focus and attention brings the entire universe to its own self realization. How cool is that? Are you getting me? Do you realize how powerful and special you are?

Affirmation

"I am living, moving, and having my being in LOVE. All of my needs are met. Life supports me. Abundance and healing is the order of my day."

LIVING IN THE LET GO!

There is a beautiful LIGHT within each one of us that is yearning to shine through the shadows of our challenges, issues, and seeming difficulties we each are growing through.

KEY: DON"T GIVE UP!

The way to surpass them all is going within you. Meditate as often as you can. Meditation makes you aligned with the highest vision for your life. It burns through the unwanted energies and untangles the condensed thought patterns, emotional burdens of the past or unnecessary worries of the future. Key: LOVE AS OFTEN AS YOU CAN! That begins with self love. You matter most. Until you learn how to appreciate and honor yourself, you will not be able to sustain desired relationships with others that eventually lead to success.

KEY: FORGIVE AND LET GO!

Clean up the pain inside. Letting go of these negative energies, does miracles. As you forgive and let go, new creative space for unlimited possibilities opens up deep within your heart. Life flows. Awareness of your higher self navigates you towards your destiny.

AND FINAL KEY: BE YOURSELF!

I just felt like sharing these as a reminder to myself.

Affirmation

"I am living, moving, and having my BEING in GOD. Life supports me. I forgive and let go, I let go and Let God handle my challenges. I am available and fully receptive to more good than I can possibly imagine. I live in abundance, in flow of the universal all good of God. Come what may.

BEST CASE SCENARIO

How much of your waking hours do you waste on projecting the worst case scenarios in your life? If you pay attention, you notice that your mind thinks about all the fears, doubts, and worries of the future automatically because it gets filled up by negative energy bombarded towards you from the news and society.

As you start your spiritual practice of meditation, prayer, and service to others, you begin to anchor yourself more in the present moment. Feed your mind positive, inspirational thoughts hourly. Do it deliberately. Right now, think about the best case scenario that your life can become. Make this as your set point. You must shift your attention to powerful intention of activating your highest potential. You are the living biology of the highest activated potential at any given moment. The universe is awakening to its own consciousness through you. Give yourself some love today for being awesome.

Affirmation

"I am living, moving, and having my being in love. Life is magnificent. I am available and receptive to more good than I can even imagine possible. Come what may."

GET OUT OF THE TRAP

No matter how much you think you are over your past, something can trigger the old memories and get you caught up in the unresolved emotions. I battle with that myself. It doesn't happen as often, but it does come up especially when I get caught up in my Ego. That is, to fall in the trap of comparison, or relating my true value on materialism, falling for opinion of others, or just being fed up with people around me. As this happens, I observe my mind; allow my emotions to pass through without judging them. I feel them deeply, not making myself wrong for experiencing pain. Then, I catch the thoughts that are provoking them. I gently look at the thoughts and remind myself that:

> "I am not my feelings, I am not my thoughts, I am not my present circumstances. I AM SIMPLY ONE WITH GOD."

I then, think about what I'm grateful for, immediately open my heart to energy of appreciation in the present moment.

This opens the door to intense inner peace and love. I say this affirmation:

> "I FORGIVE AND LET GO, I LET GO AND LET GOD. I TRUST THE UNIVERSE."

This affirmation is truly healing for me and enables me to overcome my intense pain, heart break, and emotional turmoil with ease. Right now I'm feeling that inner peace.

Sharing my thoughts helps me anchor this peace and move on.

Affirmation

"I am available and receptive to more good than I can possibly imagine. Come what may."

HEAVEN ON EARTH

There is the world you see with the eyes. Then there is a perception of what you see BEHIND the eyes. That's all your social conditioning, opinions, thoughts, and mental patterns from your past. Finally, there is the unseen, infinite, invisible, and beautiful world BEYOND the eyes. What you can not feel or see with your senses. It's what the mystics tap into, the geniuses flourish their creativity from, and the artists manifest their masterpieces out of. It's the realm of infinite good and divine possibilities. It's where unconditional love resides, where instant healing happens, "THE ABSOLUTE BLISS". It's where ONENESS dances with the sweet music of freedom from the mind. That's where I want to spend most of my living moments in. That's what meditation allows you to bring into your daily life. To live in HEAVEN on EARTH.

Affirmation

"I am living, moving, and having my being in abundance, success, health, wealth, healing, prosperity, joy, love, and absolute peace. All of my needs are met. I am in joy."

LOVE YOURSELF

It's truly an art of living to be able to sort out people who come in your life. I believe it all starts with you though. You need to be on your own side, your own admirer, true friend, and have an authentic relationship with yourself first.

Self love is so important. This is not an Ego statement at all. How can you express love, caring, and compassion to others if YOU CAN'T HAVE LOVE, CARING, COMPASSION towards yourself? When you act out without having the consideration for yourself, you live out of integrity with your soul. You get more deeply deviated from what and why you reincarnated for in this lifetime. So, do me a favor. If you read this before your morning routine, get in front of your mirrors and say:

> *"I adore myself! I honor and care for the divine love within my heart. I am worthy and receptive of all the blessings in the world. I am grateful for everything that I have and everything that I am. I am living, moving, and having my BEINGENSS in the spirit of joy, peace, harmony, and infinite abundance. I LIVE IN A FRIENDLY UNIVERSE. LIFE SUPPORTS ME, NOW."*

SUN FLOWER MEDITATION

This is a meditative thought: Take a deep breath, and slowly exhale. Do this couple of times until your focus is just on your breath and my writing. You may have to read this couple of times. As you are reading this, imagine the sun, seeing its beautiful shiny light and feeling its warm energy on your entire body. Open your heart and invite the sun energy into your heart. Each time you breathe in, feel that the sun is nourishing the cells in your blood and clearing the oxygen that is floating in it. Now take a deep breath, HOLD IT! Hold it until it becomes a bit challenging to hold. Say:

> "ALL OF MY NEEDS ARE MET, I LIVE IN A FRIENDLY UNIVERSE, DIVINE HARMONIZING GOOD AND ABUNDANCE IS THE ORDER OF MY DAY, I AM LOVE IN ACTION."

As you exhale your breath, feel the sun energy penetrating every cell of your body. Here is your task today: Go outside and stay in the sun for 20 min. Meditate on it with this writing. Then, go buy some SUNFLOWERS, hold them, feel them, touch them, smile at them, and put one on your heart. Send out a prayer of PEACE AND LOVE for the entire humanity with it. Keep one and give the rest away as a gift to anyone you like.

FORGIVE:
FOR-GIVE OR GIVE-FORWARD

Forgiveness is the most powerful act of courage. It allows you to clear out any stagnate energies trapped in your physical, emotional, and spiritual bodies. To FORGIVE is to "Give Forward" or "For Give" part of yourself hidden deep in your heart. As we approach YOM KIPPUR,

"I forgive and I ask forgiveness from every person, every being, in time and space who is karmically connected to my present conditions. If anyone has hurt me or harmed me knowingly or unknowingly, in thought, word, or deed, I freely forgive them. And, if I have hurt anyone or harmed anyone knowingly or unknowingly in thought, word, or deed, I too ask for forgiveness. MAY ALL BEINGS BE HAPPY, MAY THEY BE PEACEFUL, MAY THEY BE FREE."

Affirmation

"I forgive and let go. I let go and let God. I am living, moving, and having my being in peace, joy, abundance, success, healing, harmony, and absolute bliss. I trust the universe."

DEPRESSION GONE!

Depression is clogged up energy that is unable to be expressed. What are you trying to express? What is your soul yearning to create? Why are you holding back on those creative instincts and intuitive thoughts guiding you? Ask yourself these questions and allow the answers to reveal your path in life. Do the little things AS IF they are the most important tasks in the MOMENT. Be present to your heart beat, acknowledge your beauty, pay attention to how your body works, smile often, and talk only when you have something nice to say, and give yourself LOVE. Acceptance of who we are is the first step to personal transformation. Are you WILLING?

Affirmation

"I am willing and receptive to express my genius. I am available to all the creative ideas in the mind of universe to express through my life, as my life. I trust myself. I am worthy. I give and receive abundance of wealth through circulating my talents. Life supports me. Joy is the order of my day. Peace reigns supreme."

WHY ME?

As human being we tend to carry a lot of guilt from the past, having so many expectations from ourselves first and from others as well. When your mind starts asking "WHY ME?" kind of questions, that's an indication that you've been inoculated with FEAR, be on a look out for this energy sneaking up on you. Some of us spend an entire lifetime figuring out who to blame for our problems. This is such a waste of energy and dis-empowerment. I catch myself often getting trapped in my own mental prison. "SO WHAT, NOW WHAT?" is the question I ask myself. "HOW CAN I TURN THIS AROUND?" is a much better replacement for "WHY ME?" The ways to clear these energies are through real forgiveness and that starts by forgiving yourself. It's actually harder to forgive oneself than another being. It takes real COURAGE! I know you have it; otherwise you wouldn't be reading this thus far.

So, are you going to start investing ALL of your time and resources on yourself to break FREE from your mental trap? IT'S ALL UP TO YOU! I WILL SUPPORT YOU every step of the way. THE FINAL DECISION IS YOURS THOUGH! ARE YOU WILLING?

Affirmation

"I let go and let the universal love energy to handle my life. I am courageous, loving, compassionate, and kind to myself. I forgive and ask forgiveness from every person, every being in time and space who is karmically connected to my present conditions. I am available and receptive to more ABUNDANCE, SUCCESS, PROSPERITY, JOY, and BEAUTY than I can ever imagine. Come what may!"

WHAT'S YOUR HABIT?

Get in the habit of spending few minutes' right when you wake up to invest in yourself by saying a GRATITUDE prayer. Cultivate your mind with positive thoughts, affirmations that empower you regardless of whatever is going on, regardless of how life seems to be mis-treating you. The way to come out of your challenges is to go within, meditate, and make yourself available to that which has not revealed itself to you yet. The answer to our challenges does not come from the world of outside circumstances.

Today, I'm committed to make a mighty difference in our world, to be available and receptive to more good, more love, more joy, more abundance and success, more healing and health, kindness and compassion, and finally peace. WHY? Because the more I AM, the more I have to GIVE AWAY...the key is GIVING it ALL away.

Affirmation

"I am living, moving, and having my being in inspiration. I focus on all my blessings today. I am available and receptive to more miracles and abundance in my life than I can even imagine possible. I welcome them, come what may."

FROZEN SHELL

You live in an infinite field of quantum energy, field of infinite possibilities. It's beyond time and space. If you notice, everything in your life has been transitory. All the past events, ups and downs, whatever you've experienced up to this very second that you are reading this note, has been transitory, a cyclical change. Our lives are eternal, no beginning, and no end. Change is the only certainty we have. With change, comes opportunity. With opportunity, there is always a new beginning. Right here, right now, you can expand your consciousness and go beyond the frozen shell of your Ego, melt down the chains of the past sufferings, and step into the NOW. Take a deep breath, feel your connection to this very moment, welcome the necessary changes that will uplift your spirit to go beyond your challenges. Everything you've ever hoped, dreamed, prayed, and asked for is ALL WITHIN YOU. You've got it all. Find your sweet essence underneath the false illusion of your existence.

Affirmation

"I am living, moving, and having my BEING in infinite opportunities that support my life. I let go of that which no longer serves me, welcoming change. With an open heart full of love, I hold the space of the eternal NOW. I am blessed and a blessing to myself and others. I am available and receptive to unlimited ABUNDANCE, SUCCESS, WEALTH, HEALTH, JOY, LOVE, PEACE, AND MIRACLES than I can even imagine, Come what may.

NEVER ALONE

Being ALONE is way different than feeling 'LONELY'. When you are comfortable in your own skin without any attachments to what others may think of you, you'll start to realize that you are actually never ALONE. There is an innate energy of love always vibrating through the fibers of your body. You'll see yourself beyond the physical body and that in itself becomes your own perfect companion. You always have your next breath to count on, always there for you without expectations. In your deepest ALONE moments, you'll realize that the YOU that feels Alone, is just a vessel, passing the entire existence through its own awareness in order to go beyond separation from it. Take a deep breath, feel your heart beat, love yourself. You are one with everything that ever was, always IS, and will be FOREVER.

Affirmation

"I am whole, perfect, and complete as I was created. I recognize my divine awesome self, connected to the presence that is always nurturing me. I am living, moving, and having my being in love! I am infinitely abundant, passionately in joy, completely healthy, and deeply peaceful! Life supports me. I am available and receptive to more miracles than I can ever imagine possible. Let it role into my awareness."

GOSSIP OR PRAISE?

The second you start talking about somebody behind their back you have completely dis-empowered yourself and fall out of integrity with life. Observe the underlying pleasure you are taking, either deliberately or subconsciously. It's the work of your Ego feeding itself on lower energies of lack, limitation, jealousy, fear, competition, unworthiness, and frustration. This will result in lowering your immune system. It will also match you with the vibration of those mentioned qualities and create more of them in your life's circumstances. Why would you want to create this for yourself? STOP the GOSSIPS.

You can praise and communicate with someone directly. Share your feelings or you can simply bless them goodbye out of your life. Bring in the energies of love, appreciation, kindness, compassion, joy, healing, and peace. When you match yourself to these vibrations and stand your ground in awareness, YOU'LL CREATE a more empowering reality in your life's circumstances. The choice is yours. Master your mind and you'll live in bliss.

Affirmation

"I am living, moving, and having my being in bliss. I acknowledge my divinity, honoring my integrity, and knowing my oneness with life. As I empower myself and observe my thoughts, I empower and bring everyone else UP with me. I am available and receptive to more abundance, wealth, health, love, joy, success, creativity, prosperity, and beauty than I CAN EVEN IMAGINE. COME WHAT MAY!"

LAST DAY

*"I WILL LIVE THIS DAY AS IF IT WAS MY LAST.
AND IF IT'S NOT, I SHALL FALL TO MY KNEES
AND GIVE THANKS"*

...will you live this day through the activation of
your Soul's highest potential? Three things will
help you out on doing this: Utter your words
with INTEGRITY, open your heart to LOVE, and
be in the state of GRATITUDE in every moment
by moment. INTEGRITY, LOVE, GRATITUDE ...

... I will live this day as if it was my last!

Affirmation

*"I am a living biology of the cosmos. My life is divine. I am
living, moving, and having my being in ABUNDANCE. Joy is
the order of my day. Peace reigns supreme in all of my
activities. Prosperity knows my spiritual address. I am
available to more Good than I can possibly imagine. Come
what may!"*

REFLECTION

Take this very moment to reflect within ... as you start a new beginning, allow yourself to create a space of awareness. There is an infinite energy of love right here where you are reading this post. I don't know what you are doing: you're on your phone, computer, just woke up, it doesn't matter - Your conscious awareness to uplifting your spirit and allowing a split second for your soul's purpose to come through is what I'm interested in. As you take your next breath, I invite you to feel every cell of your body be enriched with healing energy of unconditional love, forgiveness, and gratitude. I intend to raise the vibration of your auric field through this focused attention and divine intention. As I'm dwelling in the energy of peace, I radiate and give away everything I'm feeling. I am channeling these words directly to you and your higher self:

> Joy, compassion, harmony, abundance, prosperity, health, and wealth with harmonizing goodness is the order of the day for entire humanity.

With gratitude, I release these words in the web of our existence and allow it to cultivate, activate, express, and manifest for the good of ALL GLOBAL SOCIETY...and so it is Amen. Breath out.

Affirmation

"I forgive and let go. I let go and let God to handle all the details of my life. I am living, moving, and having my being in complete joy, abundance, health, healing, and prosperity. Unconditional LOVE is the fuel for my existential BEING. MY SOUL IS ON FIRE and emanates beauty everywhere."

---

126 - BEAUTIFUL SOUL

How can I be more of my Authentic, higher Self? Great question to ask when you get to the point of frustration and want to give up. There are so many challenges in life that tests you to your limits. Watch out for the negative energies of people you associate with. They have a tendency to pull you down real fast. You must intentionally feed your mind positive thoughts and raise your vibration above the lower frequencies so that you rise above them. The confirmation you are looking for from the outside world to tell you 'who you are and what you must be doing' is an illusion. You are meant for a great, divine destiny that is only manifested through self realization, meditation, and unconditional love towards yourself. Don't allow other people's judgment shut you down. Ignore and move on. Commit to spend time and energy in yourself everyday for harmonizing the creative energy of your beautiful SOUL.

Affirmation

"I am a creative, kind, loving, beautiful, ever expansive, receptive, endlessly abundant, happy, plentitude, and peaceful individual. All of my needs are met at every level of my existence. The universe supports me. I say YES to life."

STARTING NEW

Start of a new day, a new beginning. It always starts with you. How you prepare your consciousness the first thing in the morning is by spending few precious moments, acknowledging your greatness, nurturing your mind with positive- affirmative thoughts, and going deep WITHIN your heart to tap into your true essence, LOVE. As you make this a simple practice, you become more in tune with the natural FLOW of life, you realize that you have already arrived to your destination because you are connected to the NOW. Every experience becomes a spiritual adventure. Every encounter with another human being becomes a journey into SELF discovery. Cultivating seeds of success and growth begins right where you are. You don't need to rely on any external factor or guidance. All you need is right there within you.

In this very moment, I'm holding you in higher vibration of love, joy, peace, abundance, success, and compassion. Inviting you to LET GO of your past. Allowing you to be present with life. You can do it! You have a mandate to be happy.

Affirmation

"I show up to life with an open heart. My life is one with the infinite life of the cosmos. I attract and allow abundance, success, health, wealth, happiness, love, joy, peace, compassion, and kindness into my life because that's who I am."

MYSTIC JOURNEY

I'd like to take you on a mystic journey in these very few lines. As I'm sitting right here listening to my meditation music, I'm tuned into the energy that's beating my heart. My breathing is really slow and deep. I can follow the path of each oxygen molecules entering and exiting my body. Please take a conscious deep breath right now; you are now connected to my consciousness which is intentionally rising your vibration from lower frequencies into higher. I'd like you to read this post couple of times allowing the words taking over your subconscious mind. There is so much love in this space; the only energy I feel is love, surrounding the spaces in each atom, molecule, cells, and tissue of my body. I see and feel a brilliant light passing through this space and emanating inward like a spiral and outward beyond my local space.

When you close your eyes and have read this few times, focus on the center point between your eyebrows. Take a deep breath and allow your attention fall to the peripheral (side) of your visual field. Like a diver who's going to jump off of the diving board backwards in an infinity pool of beauty and peace, step to the edge of the board, take a deep breath and dive energetically backward into oceanic space of your kindness. Feel the love energy washing over your entire body, cleansing the dense fear and worry frequencies surrounding you. The ocean of eternal love you released yourself into is pure AWARENESS. You just shifted the content of your awareness to absolute bliss. We are ONE body, ONE mind, ONE SOUL traveling into infinity together, NOW, forever, expanding. Feel your greatness and trust yourself. Enjoy the journey my friend. Namaste.

Affirmation

"I release myself in the oceanic field of my loving consciousness. The universe is infinite, flowing gently through the body of my life. My life is the reflection of cosmic order, peace, harmony, abundance, prosperity, healing, and absolute joy. I Am FREE in this very moment, expanding and stretching the energetic field of my BEING."

BEYOND THE WORDS

Where ever you are, I know the energy behind these words is going to serve you well, because they are being expressed from a deep space of love and healing energy. They are becoming form from the infinite source of where our thoughts originate from. Your beautiful eyes are picking up the light from the screen and your intelligent brain is giving them meaning. However, it's your Soul that's smiling as it is connected to mine in consciousness, simultaneously having the understanding that we are really ONE body of BEING in the inter-web we call the UNIVERSE.

Slow down your breath, slow down your thoughts, and take each word to your heart. The intention for self realization is to make you aware of your greatness, of the power already embedded within your Soul's character, as your inheritance. Your guidance comes through many different forms or channels, one being this post right now. It's meant to inspire you to take the next step for your inner growth. Whatever is pulling you towards what you've been yearning to express, listen to it. Honor it, trust it, and appreciate it. Your mind and knowledge are the tools that lay the pathway in order for YOUR MASTER HEART to express itself uniquely AS YOU!

Affirmation

"I am free to express myself through the desire of my heart. My intention is pure, my words are powerful. With all confidence and clarity, I walk the inner journey of my soul and create a world of love, joy, peace, abundance, prosperity, health, kindness, compassion, harmony and beauty for myself and everyone else around. LIFE SUPPORTS ME."

WHERE ARE YOU?

By the time this message reaches you, you've taken hundreds of breaths, thought thousands of thoughts, and have experienced so many different emotions. Perhaps you are contemplating the meaning of life, or setting a goal for future. Perhaps you are stuck in your past, feeling regret. Or perhaps you are excited about the future, looking forward for something great to happen. You may be in love or searching for love, happy or searching for happiness, maybe you are sick and tired of being sick and tired of your LIFE stuck in the same place bumping into problems over and over. Where ever you are right now is divine. The entire universe has evolved into cosmic order, manifested in this precise moment into its own awareness as your life, as your being, and as YOU. Did you get that?

Take a deep breathe and allow a split second of stillness enter your consciousness right now. Contemplate your enormity, the vastness, and the infinity you are. Read in between the lines here. Focus on your breath. As you inhale, experience your connection to the presence, and as you exhale, LET GO of any mental idea of who you are, where you are in life, and what your challenges are. Take another deep breath, feel the love energy surrounding you, lighting up the fire of inspiration, passion, and compassion deep in your heart. "There is something within you that KNOWS, and KNOWS IT KNOWS THAT IT KNOWS." Connect to it. Feel it. Embrace it. Make it the primary focus of your awareness.

Namaste

Affirmation

"I Am ONE with my source. I KNOW AND KNOW THAT I KNOW. I AM JOY, LOVE, PEACE, ABUNDANT, PROSPERITY, AND DIVINE. I AM BLESSED AND A BLESSING TO THE WORLD."

IN TUNE

This is a direct message to you as a reader, the receiver of this high frequency energy that is embedded in love, joy, and quality of peace coming directly from a source of high vibration that is right there deep within your own heart. If it resonates with you, it means that it's activating your highest potential, re-connecting you back to the source of all that there is, unconditional love, your true nature and being.

Take a deep breath and feel all of your needs met. Your body needed oxygen, and you got plenty of it. Your mind also needs fine tuning in order to become vibrationally receptive to the beautiful song of a friendly universe, the one that is ABUNDANT, KIND, and in HARMONY. You are stepping in this field of consciousness right now, and being encouraged to keep reminding yourself of the truth of your wholeness throughout your day, coming back to yourself as you get caught in the drama of your life. Practice re-connecting back to yourself. Breathe in LOVE, and LET GO of FEAR. That's the key that will answer and manifest all your prayers for you! Oh, Smile my friend ... it's All Good.

Affirmation

"I am tuned to the song of my own heart. Love, joy, peace, compassion, success, wealth, healing, wholeness, happiness, kindness, beauty, creativity, peace, and harmony are the order of my day. I AM AVAILABLE AND RECEPTIVE TO MORE GOOD THAN I CAN EVEN IMAGINE POSSIBLE. COME WHAT MAY! "

THE JOURNEY

There is a PRESENCE you are ONE with, connected to, and get energized from in every moment. Your every thought of inspiration, stems from aligning yourself with this gracious energy field. You can harmonize yourself with this love intelligence that beats your heart through your intuition directly and guides you to your destiny. Fate is what life brings you. Destiny is what you do with it. You have the ability to CHOOSE infinite possibilities in any given moment, thus re-shaping the thoughts you have that leads into your action.

Spiritual practices such as meditation and life visioning can open you up to your HIGHER SELF, your SOUL, and bring forth your highest pure being into manifestation of creative thoughts and your destiny. Invest in yourself, practice, and radiate your light to the world. There is a higher PURPOSE to your existence. FIND IT!

Affirmation

"I am living, moving, and having my BEING in LIGHT. Life supports me in every second of my existence. I am available and receptive to more abundance, prosperity, health, happiness, joy, success, healing, kindness, creativity, peace, love and compassion than I can possibly IMAGINE. Come what may! "

HEAVEN ON EARTH

Underneath your thoughts and your busy mind, there is stillness, a space of tranquility that can be reached only by letting go and surrendering to the presence. It is such a beautiful place to be even if it is for just a few moments. As you breathe into this quiet, empty space, you become one with the vastness of the universe. Infinity becomes your identity and love becomes your only true nature. Judgments reside, jealousy disappears. Fear changes its face to complete and utter FAITH, compassion arises up and takes over your entire being. The oxygen in your blood stream dance to the tune of your heart beat. They kiss each cell with a prayer of peace and freedom, joy and laughter, nourishment and vitality. Each cell becomes aware of its own beauty, reshaping itself to the perfection of divine harmony of ALL that EVER IS.

In this very moment as you've read this, YOUR SOUL IS IN BLISS. Take a deep breath my friend, you've just entered the doorway to your inner truth, heaven on earth. Namaste.

Affirmation

"I love because I AM LOVE. I am one with Infinite beauty of this love intelligence that beats my heart and breathes through my every cell. I am available and receptive to more abundance, healing, peace, success, inspiration, creativity, joy, and prosperity than I can even imagine possible. Come what may!"

SOULFUL ALIGNMENT

There is a powerful energy being transmuted in this very second as I'm writing this. It's intended to share what I've felt after an hour of guided meditation. Please take a deep breath and read through this passage completely with a smile on your face.

Right here, right now, I'm aligned with the three most amazing spiritual vibrations: LOVE, PEACE, and KINDNESS. This alignment is Real and rooted deep in my consciousness. Pure Awareness and Light is overflowing through each breath. As I Am experiencing this very VORTEX of existence, I am wrapping your Soul into this loving, kind, peaceful energy that is infinite, it's deep within YOU, and is yours to keep for EVER. While you are allowing this energy to infuse your nervous system and blood flow, I'm specifically opening and blessing your Crown and Heart Chakras for the alignment of your Wisdom and Compassion. Take another deep breath and start your day in gratitude with all that is coming your way: abundance, joy, prosperity, and peace of mind. All is well!

Affirmation

"I am living, moving, and having my being in prosperity. All of my needs are met at every level of my existence. Joy, peace, abundance, love, and creativity are my assets to fulfill my purpose in life and bringing forth my divine destiny. Life supports me. I am lighted and guided in divine love."

DICHOTOMY

In the physical world of thoughts and emotions there is always a dichotomy of opposites that pulls you in different directions. Good/Bad, Sad/Happy, Poor/Rich, Love/Hate...You know what I'm talking about? During holiday times, you are more prone to be exposed to fake happiness, or "Trying" to be joyous when you are not. You may have to "ACT" it out while your heart is experiencing pain. The cultural pressures make you inhibit your authentic truth and trigger more of the pain surfacing up. If that's the case, honor yourself. This is a perfect opportunity to go beyond the duality of your existence, take a step beyond the dichotomy, and authenticate into the Truth of your being- A beautiful Soul, free of emotional and mental suffering. Free in the light and love connected into the ONENESS of universe, just allowing yourself BEING an observant of your worldly experiences through your 'conscious awareness'. These are the most important times to strengthen your spiritual muscle and explore the miracle you truly are.

Affirmation

"I am present to my feelings and thoughts. I love and trust myself with every fiber of my Being. I am available and receptive to more miracles, joy, abundance, and peace than I can ever imagine possible. My spirit shines bright and heals anything that does not belong to me."

WHAT WOULD YOU DO?

If you had to forgive and heal one negative quality, what would it be? How would your life transition once you let go of that quality? Take a deep breath; imagine a beam of light coming down from the crown of your head finding its way into your heart. Picking up the low vibration of this quality, this beam of light brightens the shadows that's been hidden deep inside you and transmutes this energy into love, self acceptance, and peace. These three sacred aspects of yourself get blocked from time to time by your daily life challenges. How would your life change if you activated these three qualities on a moment by moment decision without looking at the world giving them to YOU, without searching for them outside? This is a neutral position I like to come back to over and over again, allowing self expression and more importantly, self love embracing my life. Enjoy the journey.

Affirmation

"I am living, moving, and having my being in peace. I am available and receptive to abundance, success, health, prosperity, joy, and peace in my life. The universe supports me, in love and with grace."

TODAY, IS THE TIME

The deepest level of self mastery is coming to a point in life where you get to test your PATIENCE and COMPASSION at levels you thought were never possible. Have you noticed how your mind tricks you into self sabotage when it thinks you have nothing going for you? Have you noticed when you are caught in the difficulties of your life, you start blaming yourself, blaming others, blaming God and the world? I can certainly relate to this. Let's challenge each other to step out of the blame and take responsibility for our thoughts and feelings. Instead of pain, guilt, and shame, mastering these two human attributes creates a sense of inner peace that radiates out to the world.

Today Is the day, This is the moment, This is the TIME where I DECLARE and DECREE happiness, joy, love, peace, abundance, success, inspiration, health and healing of the heart, mind , and body by embracing OUR SOULS TOGETHER, NOW.

Affirmation

"I AM grateful and I don't have anything to complain about. I AM available and receptive to more miracles, prosperity, and joy than I can imagine possible. Come what May...."

LAST BREATH

What if today was the last day of your incarnation in this life time? How would you like to BE in these very precious moments? How much of the nonsense that we worry about would lose its negative energy and become transformed suddenly into appreciation of what JUST IS? Transforming into love! Take a moment and reflect on what I'm writing here, take a deep breath and recognize that each second of your existence is a gift to reflect and reveal your divinity through your highest soul qualities. Let go of pain and suffering of the past you have loaded on your shoulders. Feel the tension in your upper back and neck! These are the past coagulated negative thought energies stored up in your muscles. Forgive yourself for being who you were, knowing what you knew, and what you are all about now because through releasing the old thought patterns you'll be able to activate healing. Open yourself up to new possibilities.

Take another deep breath, in this very moment I'm setting you up for a fresh new beginning knowing that you have a mandate for greatness and that mandate is coming forth at this very second because you are in a field of pure potentiality and high intentionality...Relax...Let Go...Trust...Allow... and Enjoy.

Affirmation

"I am one with love, one with life, one with the universe. All of my needs are met at this very moment. I am available and receptive to more abundance, success, health, joy, love, peace, prosperity, and beauty than I can even imagine possible. Harmonizing GOOD is the order of my day."

DIVINE JOURNEY

I just came out of a deep meditation, a journey within my soul that takes me to different dimensions of being. Experiencing an amazing sense of peace right now, I touched upon that part of me that loves without holding back. As I traveled deeper within, I came across the space of HEALING and WHOLENESS, where the radiant healing energy of compassion wraps its arms around the dark spots on my soul. It's clearing any residues of pain, anger, fear, envy, and worry. It's washing away lack and limitation, thus inviting abundance and pure joy inside. I felt oneness with every sentient being in this space; also those beings that are watching over us.

My prayer is for guidance. It's for direction and clarity, for purpose and high intention of righteous living, for raising the vibration energy of every soul, experiencing life from their own unique and sacred expression. For you, the reader that has its consciousness wrapped around these loving words, being uplifted from an ordinary phenomenon into an extra-ordinary luminous state of consciousness. Know that you are divine. In gratitude, I allow these words to find their magnetic field and bless everyone on its path into eternity. Namaste.

Affirmation

"I Am That, I Am...I am living, moving, and having my being in unlimited prosperity, abundance, healing, joy, compassion, and peace. LIFE supports me. I am available and receptive to more good than I can ever imagine possible. Come what May."

RED, HOT AIR BALLOON

It's so easy to get caught up in the lower energies of regret and blame for a current situation you may be growing through. Especially when it's towards another human being who at one point you loved but that love turned into a loss or immense pain, therefore, there are still strong emotional ties with them at some subconscious level. It still happens to me personally and I see how it comes. Usually, my Ego gets caught up in comparison with someone else's life experience. If I'm not aware of that, I end up in the turmoil of automatic "Why Me" question. "Why did this happen to me?" or "Why did she do this to me"? Both of these can trigger more dis-empowering thoughts that so easily take you down before you know it. The second you catch yourself on these mental trips, take a deep breath, recognize your divinity and the higher self of the other person.

At this level, send that person a prayer of 'forgiveness' and 'love' for having been in your life to teach you a lesson. Then, imagine them as a 'Red Color Hot Air Balloon' elevating away from your energetic field into the universe, getting smaller and smaller. Eventually, disappearing in the unknown from which they came from. Now breath out visualizing a beautiful green energy leaving your breath and cleansing all of your thoughts, emotions, with your spirit. Life supports you no matter at what stage of spiritual growth you are. God Bless you.

Affirmation

"I forgive and let Go, I let Go and Let God to handle all my challenges in life. I trust the universal love intelligence to uplift my spirit and guide me to my higher path. I AM available and receptive to more abundance, success, health, peace, prosperity, healing, and compassion than I can even imagine possible. Come what may!"

THIS TOO SHALL PASS

If you are reading this right at this very moment, I know you are growing through many challenges in different life structures. You may be having a heart ache through a loss of a loved one, financial issue that add on so much worry, health dis-ease and dis-harmony that is weighing so much on your shoulder, stressing you out. You may be carrying guilt, shame, or pain from the past circumstances that you haven't resolved. Your parents may be getting old and fragile, or you may be having marital tension, relationship turmoil that seems to be getting worse each day.

Look, "THIS TOO SHALL PASS".

Remember these sacred four words. Focus your attention on one single priority in life which is your connection to your highest Self, your Soul. Channel your energy back to the positive attributes in yourself, starting with these two things: Your ability the take this VERY NEXT BREATH, and your ability to CHOOSE THE NEXT THOUGHT in your mind. Infuse these two attributes with intense love, moment by moment. As you face each unique challenge, remind yourself:

THIS TOO SHALL PASS, with a sense of gratitude for your ability to take this next BREATH, and CHOOSING TO RECEIVE THIS HEALING BLESSING of loving thought directly from me now.

... You are loved, guided, and uplifted. THIS TOO SHALL PASS.

Affirmation

"I am living, moving, and having my being in peace. I am an agent of unlimited love and beauty. My life is divine. I am available and receptive to more MIRACLES, abundance and success, health and prosperity, kindness and compassion in my life. Come what may."

HOPE AND FAITH

Don't underestimate the power of HOPE and FAITH, the two guardian angels that are your best allies at anytime during the tough times in your life. You can count on them because their energy can lift you out of the gravity of negativity; those alone moments where your mind has tied your hands in barb wires and wrapped a chain of disappointment around your neck. Hope and faith dissolve the bigotry of the world that is so desperately trying to hang on its false identity. Invite them in your heart. Bathe them with unconditional love and ask your Soul to protect you with these spiritual angels during the adversities along your path.

Today, I cultivate hope in my heart and act upon my faith with the universal love intelligence to guide me on my divine purpose.

Affirmations

"I am one with the universal presence of love. I am available and receptive to more abundance than I can ever imagine possible. My life is divine, joy overflows from my being, and compassion radiates from my heart. Prosperity and healing is the order of my day. Caring, sharing, and purposeful living is the game I'm ALL in for."

HEART AND MIND

Dear reader, I am really glad you are reading this message right now because I'm sure you weren't thinking about this very next thought I'm planting in the fertile soil of your consciousness. Are you ready? Ask yourself:

"What is the creative vision of my soul? "What is the purpose for my life?"

Now, whatever you were thinking before these thoughts, they were not of high energetic vibration. As you contemplate these thoughts, allow yourself to fall into daydream, or night dream to whatever answers your subconscious comes up with. Practice and ask yourself repeatedly all day. Anything that aligns with your heart and embedded with love is worthy for you to act upon. Take a deep breath right now, enjoy this moment; you are being loved and cared for ---Namaste.

Affirmation

"I Am love in action. I am available and receptive to more abundance and success than I can imagine possible. It's happening now, all of my needs are met, everything is happening for my good. The universe supports me. Come what may!"

WRITE YOUR OWN STORY

What is the narrative to the story of your LIFE, today? It's so important to declare what your experience is going to BE on the get go before you enter your routine responsibilities, work, meetings, and dealing with the crazy world out there. You must set your inner world up by yourself. Meaning that you decide what your experiences will be as you hold the space for transformation and spiritual growth. Are you about joy, passion, compassion, abundance, kindness, and peace? Are you going to set yourself up for excellence, generosity, creativity, integrity, and love? It's up to you to cultivate any of these spiritual qualities in the fertile soil of you consciousness before you head out in the world. There is so much negativity out there that will get you and pull you down if you are not overflowing with positive energy. That is your responsibility to seek out by meditation, prayers, affirmations, visioning, surrounding yourself with positive people, and giving (sharing your goods with others without any expectation). This is called BEING of SERVICE to another.

What is your narrative today? What is your CALLING? Answer the call of your Soul; it's time to break free and flow.

Affirmation

"I am a generous Being- living, moving, and having my being in excellence, joy, abundance, and success. I am love in action, blessed and a blessing to the world. All of my needs are met; everything happens for my good, the universe supports me. I give and share of my gifts to the world as I intend to change the world for the better. I Am, God Is."

SELF APPROVAL AND LOVE

'I LOVE AND APPROVE OF MYSELF' ... How often do you run away from yourself, not wanting to face the Real you inside your heart? As you grow up, you get slapped with so many judgments, expectations, and false belief from your parents, then friends, and ultimately the society. Then, self approval becomes obsolete. You sense the need to prove yourself to others, get into nasty competition, and wear a face mask to portray someone YOU ARE NOT! Look, enlightened living means to be in alignment with the Song of your Soul. To grow into that alignment, the first step is Self love and Self approval, even if old thought patterns bubble up making you think otherwise. You are a piece of universal love intelligence, a living biology of the cosmos becoming aware of its own presence. Just for this very moment, completely allow self love and self approval to take over your entire being. Walk in this energy field and repeat this affirmation silently in your mind all day:

I LOVE AND APPROVE OF MYSELF

Affirmation

"I love and approve of myself. I am grateful to be me, pure love intelligence radiating my kindness, compassion, and joy to the world. I am overflow with abundance. There is more than enough in my life. I am available and receptive to more miracles in my life than I can imagine possible. I trust, I forgive, I let go, and I allow the universe flow through my life in grace and with absolute dignity. Peace is the order of my day."

YOU ARE A MIRACLE

Are you stuck in a situation where your only hope to get out or resolve it is a Miracle? I'm sure a lot of us have faced something like this in our life time and many have gotten our answers, in one way or another. Are you ready for this? Here's a way for a miracle to show up in your life out of seeming no way. Think about a person or a situation you are holding a grudge with, or having animosity towards someone, or go ahead, look in the mirror and gaze into your own eyes. If there is a feeling of resentment, notice it. I invite you to call or text that person you have issues with, or hold that bitter situation in mind, or while looking at yourself in the mirror, then say:

> *"I FORGIVE AND ASK FORGIVENESS FROM EVERY PERSON, EVERY BEING IN TIME AND SPACE WHO IS KARMICALY CONNECTED TO MY PRESENT CONDITION. I AM FREE AND YOU ARE FREE".*

If you really intend to do this, if you have the courage to do this, you will be astounded by its results. BE WILLING TO RECEIVE THE MIRACLE, ALLOWING IT TO REVEAL ITSELF IN YOUR EXPERIENCE. Do this exercise for 7 days.

Affirmation

"I forgive and let go, I let go and Let God. I am available for miracles to reveal themselves in my life. I trust the universe. I give myself permission to be great, to be healthy, and to be abundance and successful, to love, to heal, and to inspire. I am peace radiating my light to the world. "

FORGIVENESS IS COURAGEOUS

How often do you intentionally sit down, relax, and get into a 'Forgiveness' meditation? This is a magical state of being where you free yourself from the past - the pain, anger, resentment, grudge, and fear you carry from others, or perhaps from your own thoughts towards yourself. Oh ya, it's very powerful.

The path to healing is through 'Self love'. In order to find your way into self love though, you've got to 'forgive'. Some say, "How can I forgive when so many awful things happened to me?" Well, what choice do you have? Can you retrograde in the past and change the events? NO! All you are doing is ruining your present moments and chocking your inner child to death every time you fall for these negative energies. It is a challenging process, however, growth, transformation, and spiritual liberation is NOT for wimps nor is it for cowards. It's for YOU, a courageous, loving being of light.

Take over your choice now and set yourself free.

Affirmation

"I forgive and let go, I let go and let God. I release the need for holding on to my past circumstances, memories, and feelings. I bless them with peace and invite the bright light of transformation into my present moment. I am abundant, worthy, joyous, successful, and free. ALL IS WELL in my LIFE."

LIVING FREE

Fear of death is one of the most prominent and primordial fears in human existence that occupies your subconscious on a regular basis. It gets to the point where some of us are living as 'DEAD' bodies floating around the planet earth, scared of what's going to happen in the future. It can paralyze you from BEING your authentic self, living in joy, experiencing life's full potential, and contributing to the world.

In spiritual practices, you die to your FEARS and LITTLENESS every single day! Meaning that you don't live life as if something will happen somewhere down the future, no, you give life everything you have now. You live from an overflow of love, abundance, compassion, peace, kindness, sharing, and creativity that is ALL WITHIN THE TREASURE HOUSE OF YOUR HEART. Don't get hijacked by your fears. They are not REAL, especially what we call death. We live in a cyclical, multidimensional, beautifully ordered, and absolutely intricate cosmos where ALL is unfolding in perfection. Trust it, Trust yourself, live in the moment, let go and forgive all of the regrets, shame, and grudges. BE YOURSELF, and LIVE FREE.

Affirmation

"I am enthusiastic about today, because that's all I've got. I am living, moving, and having my being in love, in joy, in compassion, and in peace. I let go and let God to handle my life. I live in faith. I am available and receptive to more abundance and success than I can imagine possible. Come what may! I trust the UNIVERSE."

EXPANDED AWARENESS

Do you want to change the world? If yes, at this very instance, rise above time consciousness. Take a deep breath, imagining you rising above our planet earth, viewing it from above. Go farther back, now look at it revolving around the sun, go further back and watch the sun revolving around its own planetary constellations. As you expand beyond the mental construct of time and are floating in infinite space, your consciousness is rising above your current paradigm in life, your challenges; tapping into the infinite NOW. Relax into this moment and be available to insights, and miracles - awareness to your higher self. Your Soul is calling you. There are highest qualities of love, joy, peace, health, compassion, abundance, healing, generosity and creativity that are eternally present HERE, once you are available to them, they'll find their way to express themselves as you, as your life, as your thoughts - shifting and shattering your current circumstances, leading you to evolve into your highest self.

As you change and heal spiritually through universal laws with order, you become a perfect candidate to change the world. You matter most. YOUR THOUGHTS, ACTIONS, AND REACTIONS TO YOURSELF. (Read this post one more time, become available to this expanded awareness) You are meant for greatness.

Affirmation

"I AM available and receptive to trans-formation. I am evolving into becoming more of my authentic self. Love is my nature, peace is my attitude, and prosperity is the order of my day. Generosity flows through me, kindness reflects through my deeds. I am free in this very moment becoming one with God ."

YOUR CHARACTER

One of my favorite sayings is: *'What other people think about you is none of your business. Your reputation is in the hands of others. The only thing you have control of is your own character'* ... Staying authentic and real is a spiritual practice. Bypassing your own Ego dominated thoughts and observing them rather than projecting them to the outside world is a sacred deed. As you mature into a higher state of consciousness, you no longer identify with these thoughts and you don't judge others for having theirs because they are on their own path to self realization, traveling on this earth plane, and experiencing life uniquely from a different paradigm than yours. Our main responsibility is to clear out our own inner closets, thoughts, emotions, and stay harmonized with life as it passes through us. Here is the Key:

Love yourself fully and stay in gratitude always for everything that you have, and THOSE THAT YOU DON'T HAVE.

Affirmation

"I am living from truth with my higher being. I am aligned with divine life of the universe, living, breathing, and acting through me. My character is one of love, caring, sharing, compassion, peace, healing, and joy. I am available and receptive to more abundance and prosperity than I can imagine possible. Life supports me."

I AM, KIND

Being KIND to yourself is one of the highest forms of spiritual practice. Honoring yourself in different circumstances in life, honoring the higher part of you, your SOUL. How? Monitor your thoughts and feelings. What kind of expectations and questions do you ask yourself? Are they coming from space of love or are you stabbing yourself in the back over and over and over again? Notice your multiple personalities that show up as a result of your emotions. Being aware as each come up and dis-identifying from them anchors you in a higher realm of possibilities - a higher spiritual domain, where you can find peace, harmony, balance, and a gush of inspiration for moving forward. Open your heart to know the most important being in existence, YOU!

Affirmation

"I intend to welcome the new, to be one with my heart, one with my soul, and allow the universe work its magic in my life. I am available and receptive to more abundance, healing, inspiration, and creativity than I can imagine possible. I let go and let God for a magnificent destiny to reveal itself as my life, as my living, as my giving, as my sharing, as my thoughts, and as my existence in every moment."

YOUR DANCING DNA

Wow, grateful for another day, another chance to start a new beginning. You notice each time you wake up from a beauty sleep, you are starting a new beginning in what is a timeless, space less, eternal mesh of energetic particles floating and colliding with each other into infinity? We call this our life.

As the captain of your life, focus on all the blessings you've got right now. Go ahead; don't wait until you do anything else. Here is a perfect opportunity. Take a deep breath, follow that breath down your spinal cord, and give it a bright golden color, so brilliant that it starts highlighting all of your nervous system. The light starts penetrating your various organs, tissues, cells, and finally deep down each cell you've got a special DNA molecule, woven around each atom like a spiral. It's structure is hugging each strand together, in a beautiful harmonizing close tango, vibrating with the OMM sound of creation, before everything started, the sound of creation came out of NO-Thingness, into the manifestation of divine intelligence, shaping and forming itself into you, as your life, yes you!

Take another deep breath, you've got to read this passage one more time, visualizing where I'm taking you because in this space, dis-ease, dis-harmony, lack, limitation, fear, and worry doesn't exist. It's a space of healing, love, and light, where your breath is supplying oxygen and all the essentials to your body, relaxing your thoughts while you are focused on these words that are coming from a meditative space.

I'm connected to this beautiful energy and transferring it right through the light energy, translating into words, from your eyes, into your cerebral cortex, transforming into electro-magnetic field of beautiful information that is being picked up by your SOUL. In this united field of consciousness, we are together transforming our WORD, because you are giving an agreement to my words, in turn making it into a new conversation that will shift your internal energy field. It will resonate out to the world and uplift, inspire, encourage, empower, and heal anyone that comes across this post! For this, I am so grateful and thankful and I just let it BE.

Affirmation

"I am living, moving, and having my being in God. All of my needs are met. I am divinely guided and lighted to manifest my beautiful destiny. I am available and receptive to more abundance, success, health, wealth, and prosperity than I can imagine possible. Come what may."

HEALING IN THE 'MOMENT'

Have you noticed that tension in your upper shoulders or lower back? It comes and goes with stresses of life. You may have also noticed heaviness in your heart from time to time. It feels like a dark cloud covering the sunshine that's striving to find its way through the shadows. These are denser energies that you come across with on a daily basis from your job, kids, partner, family, friends, strangers, and other human beings dis-connected from the source.

As you read the rest of this post, start paying attention to your breath. Take deep inhalations. I know it's early in the morning or you may be reading this on the other side of the world. Let's stop in the 'moment' together. The second you INTEND to stop, slow down, and notice your breath flow in your body, you are inviting healing energy to get activated within you. Behind those muscle spasms, heaviness of the heart and the pressure on your upper chest is a coagulated thought energy that is FEAR based, a fear of 'I am not good enough', a fear of 'lack', a fear of 'future', a fear of trying to get the 'approval' of others. We all have some sort of that fear show up as the Ego takes over our perception and obscures the Reality, the prism through which our Soul is meant to shine through.

You know what? That is absolutely fine because once you become aware of these fears and start replacing them with love; it'll lose its intensity. It will get released because you are so much more than the FEAR. The Truth and you essence is field of pure potentiality - Pure unconditional love disguised in flesh and bones, a powerful energy field that has no beginning and no end. Have you ever contemplated infinity? Breath in, ease up, relax, and expand your consciousness to your INFINITE nature, woven together with GRACE, LOVE, PEACE, COMPASSION, ABUNDANCE, JOY, and HARMONY. If you've read this far and have a smile on your face, your energy field has shifted. We've uplifted the universe together and changed many lives in this very second. Now, do you recognize how powerful you are?

Affirmation

"I am powerful beyond measure. I am living, moving, and having my being in God. I am divinely guided through the spirit of love and am blessed. I am available and receptive to more abundance, success, health, healing, wealth, and happiness than I can imagine possible. It's all happening now, in this very moment, I am free."

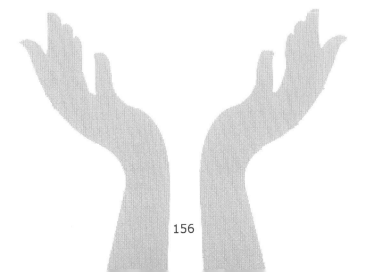

LIVING THE TRUTH

Many times in life people come in your life for different reasons. If you reflect back at your past, you realize who you attracted in your life either as a personal mate or friend. When you reflect back, look at yourself, where you were in life, what your mentality was, and who you were on a spiritual growth curve. Here is something so important not to miss; as you do this, do it with love, care, and sensitivity towards yourself and people that came in your life. As a BEING of LIGHT, you are unfolding in a constant state of 'NOW'. Your past personality selves created the blueprint to get you to this very second, where you are reading my post and realizing that you did the best you knew how, made the best decisions you knew how. The 'YOU' I'm talking about is the Soul who is unfolding through life's experiences, meeting up with challenges in order to grow and heal in this incarnation.

As you become more aware of this fact, take responsibility for your choices and inner relationship with yourself. Forgive that personality self of yours who you've been blaming and victimizing so long. Forgive the people who came in your life and left, or are still clinging on to you. You can shift them out or into your life if you get serious about your thought choices, spiritual practices, meditation, and re-gifting of your talents to the society with high intentions. This is your chance. Today is your day to make it happen. Bless your past, take a deep breath now, and know that you are always guided through the spirit of love ... Where ever you are , God IS.

Affirmation

"I forgive and let go, I let Go and let God. I am living, moving, and having my being in peace. Life supports me. I am available and receptive to more abundance, success, health, healing, wealth, and blessings than I can imagine possible. There is always more than enough. I share and give my talents back with the world, and in my sharing I get to receive."

DIVINE TIMING

Everyone has their own divine timing to come to self realization and deal with their past history. Specially the pain and suffering they caused themselves and to others. It takes courage to finally take responsibility for what you've done, what you've said, and recognizing what you've learned which is the most important part. You'll get to this point as you mature spiritually. There is no time limit because we are always leaving in the 'Present' moment. It's not until a certain level of coherent understanding and willingness has touched your heart that you will allow the truth of your being to come forth. Trans-formation requires your active participation. It's often easier for you to stay where you are because 'Change' seems difficult, it's scary to go beyond your boundaries, limiting point of views and belief systems you've picked up from the world.

What the world needs is more individuals taking responsibility for their personal thoughts, words, and choices. Getting off of our social masks, fame, fortune, comparison, envy, bigotry, stereotyping, and showing off. The world needs more humble and genuine people. Who are not looking for secondary gain in everything they do. We need more honest people with high integrity. Ones that come with clear intention to make a positive change, not gaining recognition and a boost in Ego.

Today, Notice those part of you that needs healing and is yearning to be loved. Notice the part of you that needs forgiveness. Don't run away from it. This is your day!

Affirmation

"I am living, moving, and having my being in peace. I recognize those aspects of my personality that needs healing, loving, forgiveness, and letting go. I let Go and let God to guide me on my path. I am available and receptive to miracles, healing, compassion, and love".

SENSITIVITY

I don't know about you but I've been experiencing intense amount of energies for the past few days. I'm incredibly receptive to all kind of emotional energies from people and the environment. I even feel and pick up vibes of the trees and flowers, rocks in the mountain, and animals I come in contact with. As my sensitivity has been increasing, so has my responsibility for dealing with them. I find myself more aware than ever, yearning to meditate more, to stay connected more, and do more 'light work' with energy healing. It's a very interesting path of inner growth, with lots of ups and downs.

So many times I see the down times about to happen, where my mind starts creating negative stories about life, start telling me lies about Who I Am, What I Am, Where I Am, and Why I Am. It starts making up false assumptions, bringing up false identities from the past trying to convince me of something that is not true. Be careful on how the Ego and mind operates. I invite you to get serious about a spiritual practice, especially meditation regularly. As you expand at a level of consciousness with awareness of your higher self, you will get to keep a high vibration about your TRUE Self. You cannot make up lies about your soul and inner truth. The higher, positive energies totally cancel the lower negative ones, but it's your RESPONSIBILITY to seek, go within, and get in touch with yourself. As you do, you'll gain peace and you'll lose your fears. You'll walk at a center point of the universe, just being neutral, observing life and participating in it with full on joy. I'm starting the day in gratitude and sending you lots of love, lifting your spirit to become into full understanding that ALL IS WELL.

Affirmation

"I am standing in the middle of mind of God. Everything is working together for my Good. All that I need I have within me. My life is a direct emanation of the only life that IS. I Am available and receptive to more abundance, success, healing, prosperity, miracles, and joy than I can imagine possible. Life supports me."

NEVER ALONE

How do you feel about yourself in your alone time? Do you enjoy your company or you can't stand yourself because your thoughts start to rampage in comparison, sense of separation, and feeling of void that needs something or someone from outside to fill in? Whenever you are in this alone space, notice your feelings and watch your thoughts. The more you think of yourself as whole, perfect, and complete, the more you'll enjoy your alone moments. The more you become connected with your higher Self, the more you realize that you are never ALONE, that there is a PRESENCE wherever you are, holding you in its arms, giving you tons of love. Freedom of the Self happens in the moment you are aware of your eternal, beautiful being. With this recognition in mind, notice how often you think about what other people are thinking or feeling about you, rather than how you are feeling about them. The moment you shift your energy on how you feel about them, you are empowered and can change any negative feelings to those of loving, compassionate, kind, and peaceful feelings. As you focus on the positive aspects in people, you'll tend to create more of the same positive aspects in them and yourself.

Release yourself from comparing and judging people around in order to feel true freedom of your Soul. IT IS ALL ABOUT YOU!

Affirmation

"I am living, moving, and having my being in joy. I release, and let go. I let Go, and let God. I love who and what I Am. There is wholeness, power, beauty, and compassion within me seeking to express it. I am available and receptive to more abundance, success, health, wealth, prosperity, and healing than I can imagine possible in my life. The universe supports me. Peace is the order of my day."

HEALING THE PAIN

There must be one person in your life or one situation where your heart feels pain as you think about it. As you are reading this and contemplating on where I'm about to go with this, I invite you to feel what it feels like to be 'Courageous'. Think about where in your life you had courage to face your challenges and take a leap of faith in facing them. Underneath courage, this incredible energy you posses, is the vibration of Self love. I know you have that; otherwise you wouldn't be connected to this writing and reading it right now.

It's not an accident - it's a matching of our frequencies in this very moment, guiding you into a quantum leap of higher consciousness. Open your heart and feel the Self love that's the foundation of your courage. Take a deep breath, now, go back to that one person and one situation that causes you pain, visualize it, and shrink it to a size of a 'white Dove'. Hold the Dove in the palm of your hand. Look at it so fragile and vulnerable. Feel yourself so courageous and full of Self love. As you hold on to this image, I invite you to forgive this Dove and picture it turning colors from White, to Red, To Green, and then into a bright Yellow. Feel your heart opening up and exuding Self Love towards this Dove, releasing any energy of pain, anger, grudge, and animosity you've been holding on to. As you do this, I like you to release the Dove into an empty space where it came from. Release it with both hands, allowing it to fly far away from your heart, leaving you in complete peace of mind. Bless it away, disappearing into the NO-thingness.

Take another deep breath, and repeat this affirmation: *"I forgive and let go, I let go and let God. I AM LOVE"*. God Bless YOU!

Affirmation

"I am free. I am abundantly healthy, wealthy, prosperous, and joyous. The universe supports me and guides me to my higher destiny."

THINK ABOUT THIS

You are a unique and special being with a capacity to think about what you are thinking about. As you are reading this, notice the thoughts that are going through your mind, translating the loving energy I'm sending you through my writing, feeling the words becoming actually images and experience. You are now aware that this process is happening, waking up to it. Your value and worth does not come from acquisitions of outside 'stuff', rather they come from appreciation of your innate soulful qualities; love, compassion, forgiveness, joy, peace, abundance, giving, sharing, creativity, and harmony. Recognizing these in every segment of your life's experience opens up doors of infinite possibilities to express them through you and co-create a life experience that matches up the quality you are contemplating. You are a powerful, worthy, and genius being. Hold this thought, today and focus on it, bypassing the lower energies that you come across with all day. Set up reminders on your cell phones every 3 hours, saying:

> *"I am love. right now, I have an appointment with excellence,*
> *with my Authentic Self."*

Affirmation

"I have an agreement with EXCELLENCE. My appointments with myself are about love, joy, and peace. I am available and receptive to miracles of abundance, wealth, success, and prosperity manifest in my life. The universe supports me in my intention to changing the world".

YOU ARE IT!

Let go of comparing yourself to others because every time you do, you are lowering your strength and energy. You are made up of light energy and elements of the stars, a spiritual being having a temporary human incarnation, reflecting and revealing the beauty of the entire cosmos that is within you. This self realization frees you from lower energies of jealousy, envy, being pretentious, and fake. Once you become aware of your Authentic Self, you can see the best in others because all you have is the BEST of you seeing them through THE EYES OF YOUR SOUL. You become at ease and at peace with yourself, never feeling lonely, but always in touch with your Soul.

Sometimes, there are moments of intense pain where you get caught up in past story of your life, an expectation that was not met, a promise that you told yourself and thought was real that never happened. These feelings of abandonment, lack, and void are blessings in disguise guiding you to do the inner work on yourself, forgiveness, self love, and gratitude for your life's experience. Don't shut yourself up, rather dig deep inside your heart; there is courage there, love, and compassion asking to be discovered and shared from your being to the world you perceive as real. It's what you make of it. Try seeing yourself as a healing angel in disguise, exuding light and joy everywhere you step today. You are IT!

Breathe in: *I AM*

Breathe out: *I HAVE*

Something within you Knows, and Knows that it Knows what I'm talking about.

> **Affirmation**
>
> *"I am whole, perfect, and complete as I AM. I am available and receptive to more abundance, joy, and beauty than I can imagine possible. I see life through the lens of transformation, planting seeds of success, peace, and love everywhere I go. The universe supports me. Prosperity manifests as the template of my inner being."*

THE STILLNESS

I don't know if you've ever reached a point deep within the stillness of your mind and had a chance to contemplate about your past, all the ups and downs, the dramas, those times your heart was broken, and the other times you patiently put the broken pieces back together? You observed in that stillness of your mind the different path you took and all the choices you made, some causing you joy, some major pain at the time you looked for approval, love, and inner worth. Have you ever touched that space where you see where you've come from, observing the connections of each thought, each deed, and each outer relationship? If you did, you are becoming aware of your timeless, space less essence, a being of eternal light, that is becoming AWAKE, realizing that you were always guided and protected to this point right now. Noticing, WOW, your life is a reflection of ONE Source that is in everything, everywhere, at any time, beyond your perceptions and past memories. You see your true face in the mirror of your eternal truth and magnificence glory of your being.

Take a deep breath and notice that each experience, each desire, each self reflection is part of the unfoldment of your Soul as it gets to express itself. It manifests everything that is in support to your journey here. Allow yourself this space to realize and expand in consciousness, it's an impulse pulling you towards a specific soul quality. This is a beautiful space to be, to feel, and to express through. And this journey continues my friend.

Affirmation

"I AM THAT, I AM."

NOWHERE...
NOW-(HERE) ... NOWHERE

Do the things you love without any attachment to the outcome, without striving to get somewhere or obtain something. When you completely accept what's being offered to you by the universal presence in the moment, you free yourself from acquiring the need to have more or "be someone you are not" or 'needing something to be happy'. Your full presence in the moment with 'life', embracing that everything is provided for you just like it was when you were an embryo chilling in your mom's uterus, frees you from fear, doubt, and worries of your Ego's illusion and the outside world. Let go ... Let go ... Let go ... deep breath ... you are in an infinite, eternal, ever expansive, unlimited abundant Multi-verse (multidimensional universe) that came from NOWHERE, NOW-(HERE), and returning back to NOWHERE!

Breath in, Breath out, Let Go and Let GOD.

Affirmation

"I am living, moving, and having my being in love. All of my needs are met. Everything happens for my higher good. I am cause onto my own life's experience. I embrace this power. I am available and receptive to more abundance, success, health, healing, joy, peace, and compassion than I can imagine possible. The universe supports and guides me towards my Divine Destiny."

LIVE YOUR TRUTH

Staying authentic and true to your word is the only way to invite peace and harmony in your life. Some people lie for living, or think it's just 'business'. They lie to make the deal, to cut through competition, to beat their adversary, and make profit. Until we are abiding by these norms and engaging in this mental attitude, we will not be able to create a world where the future generations can live in peace. Check mark your thoughts of identifying with external institutions holding a grip on you. Look how many times during the day you value your worth according to how much money you are making or what's in your bank account. Notice how the mock of our society has obscured or blinded your true self worth, capabilities, creativity, and genius for being a person with integrity.

Anytime you are falling for your Ego, remember that your True Self is already worthy, abundant, love, and peace itself. Monitor yourself with each breath and don't fall for the LIES! The more you remain authentic and in harmony with the flow of life, the bigger impact you'll have on changing the world for the better.

Affirmation

"I am living, moving, and having my being in God. All of my needs are met. I am available and receptive to more Good than I can imagine possible. I am peaceful and serene, allowing the universal laws of life to freely move through me. I am grateful for "NO-THING" manifesting as everything that I require to fulfill my divine destiny. With God and Love, I've got it ALL."

FROM BITTER TO BETTER

How often you get hooked to your past and feel the emotional pain of loss, hurt, or betrayal of love surfacing up, obscuring your present moment? As you become more aware through meditation and inner work, you'll go through a transition state where these past memories show up like bubbles , but they will disappear faster than they appear into space of 'NO-Thingness' from which they came from because of your high state of consciousness. You immediately catch yourself being caught in the thoughts rather than staying in déjà vu for long period, thus missing on the eternal now. Coagulated negative thought energies are healed through Self Realization and forgiveness, both requiring courage to win your own arguments about self doubt, limitations, social beliefs, lack, separation, and un-worthiness. As you invite eternal spiritual qualities in your life and practice them, you become the magnetic field to which the spirit of love, joy, peace, abundance, compassion, healing, and kindness recognizes itself as YOU. You are a pioneer of infinite possibilities! Recognize your greatness and move with confidence. You are IT.

Affirmation

"I am living, moving, and having my being in now. Divine guidance, creativity, love, joy, and peace are my best friends today. I am available and receptive to unlimited goodness flow through my life. Healing of the heart, clarity of the mind, and awareness of my soul is my starting point. The universe supports me. I am blessed and a blessing, circulating my talents, gifts, and positive vibes to uplift, heal, and change the world for the better."

BEING FOR OTHERS

"Serve the needs of others and all your own needs will be fulfilled". These words have so much merit. They truly resonate with my fundamentals. I do feel the happiest when I'm helping someone and have created a context for transformation. The contend of my conversation flows naturally through the state of my being. Authentic communication and connection is created through bypassing your own Ego, realizing its energy working 24/7 in you, yet by observing it you'll surpass its different disguises. I'm going through some deep changes myself and as different layers of Reality reveal itself to me; I become more convinced on how important it is to constantly BE conscious about your awareness. There is a universal energy, vibrating through and as YOU. Pay attention to it with this next Breath you are taking. The closest place you'll feel it is in your heart, beating continuously, in movement and action all the time. Go a layer deeper and you'll see your Divine Self translated into love, smiling back at you. It's a vibration; bypass the word 'LOVE' itself. It's a magnetic pull of quarks and specks of "NO-THING" energy field dancing together, moving forward, yet very still. When you choose to be in service to others, BE there for them from this incredible space. Release all doubt. Allow the presence to pure it's blessings through you.

> **Affirmation:** *"I tap into my creative genius today. Staying focus on my pure intention, I allow life to express itself through me. I am available and receptive to more LOVE, JOY, ABUNDANCE, HEALING, and MIRACLES in my life than I can imagine possible. My life is the life of God. I AM peace in service to others, shining my light where ever I go."*

HARMONIZING GOOD

We each have a responsibility to look deep within our lives and see what's working, what's not working, and how we can change our conversations in order to have a positive effect on our surroundings. Many times, we point fingers at others or certain people become scapegoats for our own lack of judgment. Where we need to step up to the game, yet we don't have the courage to say what's in our hearts. Wise decisions and pure intentions that are aligned with universal laws of peace, compassion, unity, and liberty always prevail the lower, hateful, blaming, gossiping conversations that drag us deep into the gutters of our society. For the world to change, we need to change from within. Courageous being that leads into pure intention will result in a kind and justice world where our future generation can live in harmonizing good.

Affirmation

"I take responsibility for my inner dialogues, thoughts, words, and ultimately my actions. I open my heart to love and extend gratitude for every blessing in my life. I am available and receptive to more good than I can imagine coming my way. With courage, I choose to circulate my good for the benefit of the whole."

ALONE OR LONELY?

Be able to tell the difference between being Alone and feeling Lonely. Feeling lonely comes from a sense of lack. This happens when you are disconnected from your true essence, not able to be in touch with your higher self. Where you have pain inside your heart and don't know where it comes from. It's not a very good space to be in because it hurts and your only way out is to go deep within in order to heal what is the root of that separation.

In contrast, BEING ALONE is a GIFT. It's where healing of the heart takes place. It's a quiet space of self realization and internal peace, away from the drama of the world outside, a blissful opening to knowing yourself. Getting in touch with your true essence and realizing that you don't need anyone or anything to be happy, because you are directly in touch with the universe itself, and that my friend, is found only in your ALONE moments where you are self reflecting, meditating, and giving rest to your brains cells. Is your Soul smiling during your ALONE moments or are you constantly searching to fill up a void that needs to be healed in your heart? Good question to ponder about.

LEADERSHIP

Leadership is the ability to influence others. How you influence others is a direct relationship on how you are taking care of your own inner household. What thoughts you are allowing to navigate through your mind? How open is your heart to love? Are you letting go of your past and processing out the pain you've been holding on to or you are masking a happy front with a broken heart behind it?

You become an effective leader as you focus your attention to the deepest areas of your life with an intention to bring your highest potential as a gift to humanity. These are eternal, Soul qualities that are vibrating at higher frequencies from the mock of human experience domain, Compassion, Appreciation, Peace, Kindness, Sharing, Healing, Bliss, Beauty, Harmony, Abundance, Joy, and Creativity. Are you really in integrity with your Soul or do you fall deep when you allow negativity effect your core being? Leadership is a lifelong process, a manifestation of your commitment to your highest Self and a practice of discipline in being of service to others. Here is the awesome news: You have the ability to fulfill your creative vision that is the direct emanation from the cosmos and can lead others to greatness, because you are greatness!

IT IS YOU!

The beautiful and amazing life you are seeking is the direct reflection of your beautiful and amazing higher Self. Tapping into your awareness that you are more than a body and flesh, more than challenging life experiences, more than the sum amount of your current circumstances and situations that have pushed you into a corner, perhaps clouding your perception as to WHO and WHAT you are.

Take a deep breath; I just finished an hour of meditation process that started with healing the body, then traveling to UNCONDITIONAL self LOVE, opening up to this love through act of FORGIVENESS. I really focused on forgiving myself and I know you probably have realized that the toughest person you deal with on a daily basis is yourself. So, here is my invitation to you: As you are in this vibration right now, if you've kept on reading this far, I'm sending you Reiki, clearing out your entire Chakra systems, into the deepest layers of your subconscious mind, opening doors of opportunities through power of Self forgiveness in order to gain clarity of the mind, body, emotion, and your beautiful soul. As this energy is penetrating your entire field, I see a resonating light surrounding you, and then I see it going through you. This eternal, healing light which surrounds you and goes through you, is flowing IN, THROUGH, and as YOU --- IT IS YOU!

With this in mind, see yourself as an abundant, whole, perfect, kind, generous, compassionate being, free in this moment from any self JUDGMENT, GUILT, and SHAME. Free from the anxiety of the future and the pain of your past. Free in this instance, flowing through an ocean of love, peace, joy, success, prosperity, and harmonizing good.

Tonight is PassOver. For all of my friends who celebrate and really for the entire globe, I send out this prayer of freedom from the Ego, from the old residues of lack and limitation, and bring forth a clearing of our perception, to reach OUR HIGHEST POTENTIAL AND CARRY OUT OUR DIVINE DESTINY, WHICH IS TO REFLECT AND REVEAL THE MAGNIFICENCE OF THE COSMOS ACCORDING TO OUR UNIQUE PATTERNS. WITH THE HIGHEST SENSE OF GRATITUDE, I RELEASE THIS VISION AND PRAYER INTO OUR WORLD … HEALING IT RIGHT NOW!

Affirmation

"I am blessed and blessing to the world. I am living, moving, and having my being in God, in joy, in peace, in prosperity, abundance, and absolute bliss. My life is divine. Healing is the order of my day. I am available and receptive to more miracles than I can imagine possible. I am grateful for having all of my needs met and thankful for being in service to humanity."

WHY COMPLAIN?

Be aware of one habitual complain you have as a usual pattern in your mind today. There may be more than one, but only focus on the most nagging one. The second you capture that thought, take a deep breath and notice there is a part of you that needs to be acknowledged and loved. It's been somehow neglected or imprisoned behind your thoughts of worry, lack, guilt, I'm not good enough, or I need more to be happy. You know exactly what I'm talking about. Breath in, just be aware that these energies come and go within your energy field. By simply observing and acknowledging them through your awareness, these feeling will fade away and heal. The key is MEDITATION. Don't judge them; don't get upset when they show up. Always fall back to your spiritual power of discernment, choosing what your inherent nature is. I invite you choose Love, Peace, Compassion, Joy, and Laughter. Allow, embrace, and then give it all away to someone that needs you.

Affirmation

"I am love in action. I am living, moving, and having my being in the spirit of peace. Joy is my nature. Creativity oozes through me. Divine healing takes over my life. I am available and receptive to miracles showing up in every area of my life. Today is a beautiful day. I attract and allow abundance, success, health, wealth, happiness, kindness, beauty, and harmonizing good into my life because that's who I AM.

I AM THAT, I AM..... Namaste."

IT TAKES COURAGE

It takes courage to raise above the fears and anxieties of your current life experiences and go beyond them even if you have to use your IMAGINATION. Imagination is the angel of God, bringing you the energy of the impossible and pulling you towards the gates of I'm-possible. It takes courage to wake up with an attitude of gratitude, even if you have no reason to be grateful for. Just the fact that you are intending to shift your energy from victim to victory, from depression to expression of your soul is enough to take you from resistance and generate flow. You can do this. It's just a shift in your perception and a willingness to set in motion your inherent, powerful, joyful, compassionate, loving, abundant, peaceful, and creative higher self that knows, and it knows that it knows, in order to dissolve the pain and sufferings of your heart. It needs your permission, it needs your courage, and it needs a bit of an enthusiasm. ARE you up for it? Are you willing to shine and stand tall right here, right now? Why waste time? I think this is your moment, right now. Go for it!

Affirmation

"I Am that, I am. I am living, moving, and having my being in love. My life is the direct emanation of the only life that exists. I am available and receptive to more abundance, prosperity, and health than I can ever imagine possible. Joy is the order of my day. Peace is direction of my heart. Life is good. I am grateful for absolutely NOTHING that manifest into miracles in every areas of my life."

PERSONAL RELATIONSHIP

So many of us struggle with personal relationships, at one point in your life, you thought you were in love with someone. I don't doubt that. Love is a state of being that is inherent in all of us. It's our natural state of being. On a spiritual journey, your definition of love starts to shift. As you grow and get to know yourself deeper, your tendency to be completely neutral in love expands.

Many times, people who are in our lives don't catch up in this evolution. You take on a path of personal discovery and find deeper aspects of yourself, connect with your purpose in life, and become in tune on a vibration that is completely off tune with your partner's. If there is no spiritual partnership, growth, deep connection, support, and an aligned vision together, the relationship will dissolve and dis-integrate from each other. It will not continue. No one is to blame. This is the nature of our human beingness evolving on our course, meeting different angels in our lives that give us what we need at that specific time period. Pointing the finger of blame and judgment on your X-partner or one to be X soon is an immature way of looking at this phenomenon. The message this has for you is to discover avenues for forgiveness, discovering ways to expand and grow, discovering to be more loving and compassionate as ever before, even if it has to do with letting go of what no longer serves you. You can heal your life, your relationships, and other people once you open up to healing yourself and loving yourself first. Have Self Worth and trust the universal source of love to guide you to your destiny.

Affirmation

"I am living, moving, and having my being in love. I am available and receptive to more prosperity than I've ever imagined, experienced, or manifested. My life is divine. I trust the universe to guide me on my path, pull me towards a vision of healing and changing the world for Peace, Harmony, Compassion, Kindness, Abundance, Success, Health, and Wholeness. I am totally grateful and thankful for NO-THING that MANIFESTS as All the miracles in my life. I am blessed and a blessing to the world. And so it is. Amen."

HANG ON

When your back is against the wall and you feel like your entire world is crumbling right in front of your eyes, hang on. This is the time to strengthen your faith in the power that created you and took care of you before you were even born from eternity. To get deep down in touch with your Soul, self reflect, meditate, and release yourself to the unknown. Surrendering to the higher order of universe doesn't mean to "Give Up". It means to give up unnecessary control of the Egoic mind and allowing the energy of life to flow in every area of your life. It means to discern between thoughts that are valid and distinguishing between invalid, fear based thoughts that are coming from lack of self love, unworthiness, pain, suffering, and scarcity consciousness. Once you reach this distinction, there is a space of letting go into the Infinite Intelligence of that which is eternal, Real, and is operating in, through, and as YOU- we call this "LIFE". Swim downstream through the current of higher order, harmony, and peace. This is what you can choose to Be, Do, and Have even when you feel you have lost it all. Strive to get out of your challenge by healing what's going on within your heart, mind, and Soul. The universe will support you. Hang on my friend.

Affirmation

"I am available to more prosperity, healing, and love than I've ever experienced, imagined, and manifested. Life supports me. I live in a friendly, abundant universe. I forgive and let go of any hindrance to this truth and allow my life to reflect and reveal the glory of the cosmos. Peace is the order of my day."

MELTING AWAY

It's so difficult to witness people you love getting old and melting away right in front of your eyes. One of the ways I deal with this situation is to remind myself that we are spiritual beings having a temporary human incarnation and there is more to the old, frail body. There is the soul behind the illusion of our physical self, an eternal, infinite energy of love. When I view my loved ones through this prism, it enables me to see only the beauty behind the illness, the pain, and the fragile face. Still though, no matter how deep I look at it, it hurts me!

THE GLORY

Can you see the beauty and the glory in your life? As you grow into spiritual maturity through daily practice, obscurities fade away and a clear vision of who you are, what you are, and why you are here to do what you do becomes totally apparent. You go from self-centeredness into being centered in the Self. After you read this, set aside 5 minutes and close your eyes. Do NOTHING. Just sit or lay down in a comfortable position and breath.

Affirmation

"Infinite, invisible good manifests as all my needs get met. I am living, moving, and having my being in love. I trust the universe. I am available and receptive for miracles to show up in every area of my life. In gratitude, I just let it be."

YES, I CARE

You live in a beautiful field of abundance and infinite possibilities for your life. There is so much to the depth of our universe that is not picked up simply by our senses. It requires tapping into deeper realms of your own inner wealth that is only possible through meditation. Connecting with your higher self allows you to shift perceptions. Everything is Perception. As you change the way you look at things in your life, you'll see the circumstances shift and challenges dissolve in the way that supports you. To walk in this direction requires persistence on your practice and a WILLINGNESS to change the sail of your ship towards a magnificent destiny. Your destiny is not out there, it's in the depth of your heart and Soul. It's waiting to be discovered and recovered from the illusions you've fallen for, from the pain and suffering you've picked up from your mis-perceptions, dis-eases, and dis-connection from the source. The path to healing and acquiring inner peace is through your perception. It's through becoming overflow with the bank of your consciousness. True wealth is inter woven in between the molecules of your DNA, swimming in the midst of your blood stream, feeding your every cell with the energy that is connected to astral bodies. Your entire BEING is ONE with the Universe. Take this on as a new perception and walk with the knowing and the wisdom that YOU ARE IT my friend.

Affirmation

"I am one with love, one with the universe. All of my needs are met. I am available and receptive to more prosperity than I can imagine possible. My life is divine. Healing is the order of my day. I am living, moving, and having my being in abundance, plentitude, and success."

HOPE

Here is a healing energy towards humanity, towards the dis-ease and suffering of the world. To uplift anyone who is going through difficult times and not having their legitimate needs met. As you read this, focus on a grand vision you have for your life, something that is beyond your imagination. Pick up on a soul quality that you want to manifest more of in the world. Is it love? Is it peace? Is it abundance and prosperity? Is it compassion and harmony? Is it inspiration and enthusiasm? Is it wholeness and well being? Is it creativity and wisdom? Or is it All of them? As you continue reading these words coming out of my being from deepest state of meditation right now, realize that I'm holding the space for these qualities to manifest more of, in my life and as a united field of consciousness, connected together in this field of oneness, I have you connected as well. There is an intention set in motion right now for us living a life of significant, joy, dignity, and becoming an empty vessel to receive more blessings than we can imagine, and to be channels for hope. miracles, and change in our world. YES! it is POSSIBLE. We are doing it together.

Affirmation

"I am living, moving, and having my being in bliss. Peace is the order of my day. I am available and receptive for more prosperity than I can imagine, experience, or manifest. All of my needs are met. Everything happens for my higher good. I am grateful, thankful, and appreciative for miracles showing up in my life. I release, I let go, I allow, I receive, I share, and I give it all away. The universe supports me. I AM LOVE."

BYPASSING INERTIA

As you move and swim through life, you come across challenges and situations that test your resilience, most of the time, you think you can force your way through them or bypass, by taking a short cut. That's your Ego at work. It takes commitment to your spiritual practices and lots of forgiveness in order to stay in flow. What I've experienced is that everything happens for the best reason and there is a divine timing for it all. The most important part of existence is being in alignment with your purpose and staying authentic with it. As you deviate from your path, being willing and having an activated intention toward your vision in life, will guide you through life's challenges. There is a seed idea waiting for your YES to be cultivated, activated, expressed, and manifested as you open your heart, stand in the light of your radiant glory, and step out of the inertia that's been holding you hostage. How willing are you to live in this freedom and be one with love?

Affirmation

"I hold my challenges in the radiant glory, the infinite spaciousness, abundance and love, and the blissful peace of its own true self. I am available for more good than I can imagine possible. Healing is the order of my day. I am living, moving, and having my being in Peace, Abundance, Love, and Bliss. ALL IS WELL."

GET OUT OF DEBT

Un-forgiveness on any level creates a negative energy field in your life that resonates back as 'LACK' to the universe. When you are holding on to un-forgiveness, you are actually sending out a message that: *"This person owes me something. This situation did me wrong. There is lack in me."* What happens is that the energy you are sending out will translate as 'financial debt' and great 'resistance' to natural flow of abundance in your life. Pain, misery, depression, and anxiety are all functions of holding on to some sort of stagnant, coagulated, rusty energy in your heart and Soul.

The nature of life and universe is beauty. The flow of abundance and prosperity comes from your clear space of consciousness where it's resonating from love, compassion, and generosity. The universe responds by corresponding to its own nature when it matches up to higher Soul qualities that are inherent in your heart. So, take a deep breath right now, notice a situation or someone you have not forgiven. Realize that you need to show a bit of courage to do this because it takes guts to break away from mediocrity, from your comfort zone, from your nagging story and victimization. Yes, YOU NEED TO SNAP OUT OF IT RIGHT NOW! Haven't you had enough of that miserable story? Aren't you tired of your old BS (belief system)? You have a chance to let go right now.

Say: *"I forgive and I ask forgiveness from every person, every being, in time and space who is Karmically connected to my present condition".*

Take another deep breath, hold it, and then release by saying the sound of "AHHHHHH" ... Today is going to be a magnificent day. Stay open and receptive to amazing miracles happening in your life.

Affirmation

"I forgive and let go, I let go and let God. I am available and receptive to more prosperity, healing, abundance, success, and wealth than I can ever Imagine, Experience, or Manifest. Life flows through me in harmony and peace. All of my needs are met. I am grateful for my existence."

YOU HAVE IT ALL

For the next few seconds that you read this, let go of any anxious thoughts or fear of future you are carrying. Intend this to be a moment of calmness and peace of mind. I invite you to take a deep breath and activate the thought of *"I AM GOOD ENOUGH"*. Being more than your physical body and life experiences, this is a sweet moment to realize your Soulful quality, and eternal being of light and love. In this very moment, I want you to realize that you are extremely powerful. Do not try to get anything from the world. Happiness and bliss are states of inner being that are inherent within your Soul's character. The world outside has nothing to offer you but bunch of negative news, low conversations around how "everything is messed up". You've seen it and heard it. So many people walk in this fear based mentality. I don't deny the challenges, difficulties, and dis-eases that are so rampant in our society. Yes, they exist. So does the antidote to all of them.

Once you realize that you already have everything you need, be a distributor of love and joy. Become a portal point to express generosity and compassion. Exude abundance in your conversations. If someone says how is life? Get into the feeling tone of EXCELLENCE!

The way out of where you are is to GO WITHIN your heart and Soul. There is no way around it. Don't wait for others to do miracles for you, and don't wait for your life to change. Relax into this very second and acknowledge your strength, vigor, intelligence, wisdom, and confidence. If you cannot feel this, imagine the best case scenario of your life and go beyond where you are, pulling this energy from your future into the present moment, the only moment that exists, is here and now. Take another deep breath, use this affirmation:

"ALL OF MY NEEDS ARE MET. I AM LIVING, MOVING, AND HAVING MY BEING IN LOVE. I AM AVAILABLE AND RECEPTIVE TO MORE PROSPERITY, JOY, HEALING, AND WEALTH THAN I CAN EVER EXPERIENCE, MANIFEST, or IMAGINE POSSIBLE. I FORGIVE AND LET GO, I LET GO AND LET GOD. I AM GRATEFUL FOR NO-THING THAT MANIFESTS INTO MIRACLES IN EVERY AREA OF MY LIFE. I TRUST THE UNIVERSE".

ABOUT THE AUTHOR

Dr. Rod Pezeshki lives by this INTENTION as his vision: To love, to heal, to inspire, and to be abundantly wealthy for himself and everyone around the world in order to raise the collective cosmic consciousness. He has a Medical Degree from New York Medical College and a Bachelors of Art degree in Biology from CSUN. As an Author, Spiritual Healer, Reiki Master, Meta-therapist, and an inspirational Life coach, Dr. Rod has dedicated his life to help individuals all around the world. His purpose is to heal and to change the world for better. As an avid Hiker, Dr. Rod conducts his global healing meditation in the Caballeros Mountains daily. He holds lectures, private sessions, and guided Chakra healing group meditations regularly. He loves life and enjoys his family the most.

Other Books by Dr. Pezeshki: 'Live a Purposeful Life with Passion" and "The Loving Light Within" found on his website:

www.DrRod26.com

36896902R00115

Made in the USA
San Bernardino, CA
26 May 2019